THIS BOOK
PROTECTED
BY AN ATTACK CAT

GARFIELD © 1978 United Feature Syndicate, Inc.

JIM DAVIS

THIS BOOK PROPERTY OF

DOPPLER COLOR
FLOW IMAGING

DOPPLER COLOR FLOW IMAGING

Joseph Kisslo, M.D.

Professor
Department of Medicine
Duke University Medical Center
Durham, North Carolina

David B. Adams, R.C.P.T., R.D.M.S.

Chief Cardiac Sonographer
Department of Medicine
Duke University Medical Center
Durham, North Carolina

Robert N. Belkin, M.D.

Associate in Medicine
Department of Medicine
Duke University Medical Center
Durham, North Carolina

CHURCHILL LIVINGSTONE
New York, Edinburgh, London, Melbourne 1988

Library of Congress Cataloging-in-Publication Data

Kisslo, Joseph A. (Joseph Andrew), date
  Doppler color flow imaging.

  Includes bibliographies and index.
  1. Doppler echocardiography. 2. Heart—Diseases—Diagnosis.
I. Adams, David (David B.) II. Belkin, Robert N. III. Title. [DNLM:
1. Cardiovascular Diseases—diagnosis. 2. Echocardiography—methods.
3. Ultrasonic Diagnosis. WG 141.5.E2 K61d]
RC683.5.U5K55   1988   616.1′207543   87-21215 ISBN
0-443-08563-3

© **Churchill Livingstone Inc. 1988**

Distributed in the United Kingdom by Churchill Livingstone, Robert
Stevenson House, 1–3 Baxter's Place, Leith Walk, Edinburgh EH1 3AF,
and by associated companies, branches, and representatives throughout
the world.

Accurate indications, adverse reactions, and dosage schedules for drugs
are provided in this book, but it is possible that they may change. The
reader is urged to review the package information data of the
manufacturers of the medications mentioned.

Acquisitions Editor: *Robert A. Hurley*
Production Designer: *Gloria Brown*
Production Supervisor: *Jane Grochowski*

Printed in Hong Kong by Mandarin Offset

First published in 1988

Dedicated to
Joseph A. and Estelle Kisslo
Ruth Adams
Beth, Daniel, and Samuel Belkin
Ruth and Edward Belkin

PREFACE

Doppler color flow methods are relatively new. Few have had experience with this diagnostic approach yet many have interest in its potential use. When we began with this technique several years ago we realized there was little resource material upon which to base our clinical work. There were only a few articles showing practical examples of disorders evaluated with color flow imaging techniques. No simple explanation of the operating characteristics of these devices existed. Moreover, most of the literature was in Japanese, a language with which we have little facility.

We waited for detailed explanations to be forthcoming; none came. We hoped some of our colleagues would bring a similar volume to press and offered our help; none accepted. Meanwhile, we found enlightenment in our experience and in our conversations with others using the early prototype systems. We recognized that there were many individuals desiring a comprehensive review of the current status of color flow imaging.

This book is prepared in the simplest and most direct fashion possible. We recognize that Doppler, and particularly Doppler color flow imaging, may be an intimidating subject to some readers. We have tried to be as simple as possible in our approach. We hope that those with other opinions and/or greater knowledge will forgive our desire to keep complex things simple. We have made every effort not to sacrifice truth at the expense of simplicity. We made special effort to discuss the technical details of system operation, for we found none in existence to help the beginner.

This book is not, and has no pretense to be, a complete book summarizing all matters relating to Doppler color flow imaging. We think it is suitable for those with a strong background in two-dimensional and Doppler echocardiography. We even tried to prepare it keeping in mind that some readers may have no experience with conventional Doppler methods. There are other texts that cover these subjects, and readers should not be disappointed by the fact we did not include details of all uses of cardiovascular ultrasound. We did not have the room and there would be no buyer who could stand the expense of such a volume.

We thank the cardiac sonographers of the Duke Echocardiography Laboratory: Woody NeSmith, Diane Branscome, Judy Philips, Pat Denning, and Linda Postotnik. For years we have thought that we have the most superior technical staff in the world. Their complaints are few, dedication to teaching high, and good spirits unrelenting. These individuals spent great effort in collecting and commenting on the clinical cases presented. For their kindness to patients, their clinical skills, their dedication to teach others, and their natural joy for life and work, we thank our staff.

We also thank those who taught us so much about color flow imaging. Professor Ryozo Omoto of Saitama Medical School, Japan, helped us to recognize the potential for color flow imaging. His diligence, good faith, and friendly manner stimulated our early interest and helped us to bring this method into clinical use in our institution. We recognize the efforts of Dr. David Sahn and Dr. Jos Roelandt in helping to establish this technique in the United States and Europe.

It was Mr. Steve Leavitt of Hewlett-Packard who spent untold time and effort tolerating our ignorance, teaching us basic principles and reviewing our manuscripts for accuracy and content. We also thank him for our fellows who received his counsel.

Thanks also to Mr. Ray O'Connell and Mr. Arthur Dickey of the Hewlett-Packard Corporation who helped with our initial understanding of the principles of color flow imaging. More thanks to Mr. Paul Schrader of Hewlett-Packard and Mr. Ivan Young of Toshiba for making sure we had working equipment to prepare our clinical illustrations. Always available by phone or in person, they all helped to speed the production of this volume. Our gratitude is also extended to Joan Main, formerly with the Irex Corporation, for her early boundless enthusiasm for color flow imaging.

We extend further thanks to Mrs. Penny Hodgsen for her good humor and for translating our written words into English. Thank you also to Mrs. Jackie Smith for her diligent typing skills, no matter what her blood sugar levels!

Our further gratitude is extended to all the audio-visual staff at Duke. Miss Eleanor Johnson created the color drawings and tolerated our multiple changes. Mr. Butch Usery and his staff developed all of our film and supervised the quality control. The illustrations in this book are selected from well over 3,000 original static images!

We thank Dr. Joseph C. Greenfield, our Chief of Medicine for his support, encouragement, equipment, and opportunity to write. Other colleagues at Duke deserve special mention: Dr. David C. Sabiston, Chief of Surgery, for realizing the potential of intraoperative ultrasound; Drs. Peter K. Smith and Ross Ungerleider of our Surgery Department for taking the transducers into the operating room; Dr. James Lowe of our Surgery Department for the wonderful intraoperative photographs; Drs. Madison Spach and Jerry Serwer of our Pediatric Cardiology Division for counsel, cases, and cooperation; and finally Drs. Norbert de Bruijn and Fiona Clements of our Cardiac Anesthesiology Division for their contribution, continuing good spirits, and general excitement over just about everything. We are appreciative of the efforts of Dr. Olaf von Ramm for being Dr. Olaf von Ramm, Sylvia Hubbard for providing a method for us to process the words in this book, and John Miglin for assisting us in every experimental model.

Thank you to Mr. Robert Hurley, Editor-in-Chief, at Churchill Livingstone, as representative of our publishers. Willfully accepting a book with such abundant color illustrations has only a few precedents in medical publishing.

Our special thanks to our wives, Kitty, Lee, and Beth. Eating dinners alone was not easy for them. Our food was still warm in the oven even though we were long past our promised hour of return home for the night. We appreciate their tolerance during the ordeal and continued faith that this project was worth our efforts. Our older children, Shelly, Connie, Tony, and Andy worried a bit that we worked too hard. Our younger ones, Daniel and Samuel, just missed playing with Dad. Our then waiting to be born, Page, was the only one who kicked and fussed and refused to wait.

We finally and most specially thank our patients. No reader should forget their tolerance of our sometimes tedious examinations to obtain the best possible materials for illustration. We share their excitement for this new approach to cardiac imaging. They all hoped that their patience and misfortune would benefit others.

We hope our readers will think these efforts worthwhile.

Joseph Kisslo, M.D.
David B. Adams, R.C.P.T.,
R.D.M.S.
Robert N. Belkin, M.D.

CONTENTS

1

Color Flow Imaging in Clinical Practice

Doppler color flow mapping is a method for noninvasively imaging blood flow through the heart by displaying flow data on the two-dimensional echocardiographic image. This ability has generated great excitement about the use of color flow imaging for identifying valvular, congenital, and other forms of heart disease.

Part of the excitement engendered by color imaging is that disordered cardiac flows are more readily identified than with conventional Doppler approaches. Widespread clinical experience with this modality is limited at present, and most individuals have great difficulty in understanding how color flow images are created.

Given this situation, it appears to us that there are few introductory explanations of the technique and its applications to the clinical care of patients. Thus, the purpose of this volume is to satisfy the needs of those individuals who are beginners with color flow, those who are considering its acquisition, and even those who have only a casual interest in learning a little more about what color flow imaging is all about. The early chapters unravel the sometimes confusing Doppler principle, the very basics of Doppler methods, and the details of the creation of color flow images. There is some discussion of the operation of color flow systems followed by several chapters on the use of color flow imaging in various disease states. The volume is clearly intended as a starting place.

We hope this serves as an extension to the earlier work of Omoto and his colleagues published in a *Color Atlas of Real-Time Two-Dimensional Doppler Echocardiography*.[1] We make no pretense to cover the entire field of Doppler echocardiography. Inexperienced Doppler users are directed to the very basic explanations of conventional Doppler contained in *Basic Doppler Echocardiography*.[2] A more in-depth discussion of Doppler methodology is found in *Doppler Ultrasound in Cardiology*[3] by Hatle and Angelsen. While most of our discussions assume no detailed previous knowledge of Doppler, the fullest understanding of color flow will reside in those experienced in conventional Doppler approaches. In addition, advances in this method are taking place daily and the reader is referred to current periodical literature for developments that serve to extend or limit the use of this technique.

Understanding of color flow imaging using Doppler methods begins with an appreciation of the timing of flow-related events. In this chapter we explain the very basics of cardiac flow and introduce the Doppler principle. It forms the baseline for deeper understanding of how the Doppler principle is used to create images of moving red blood cells.

1

Important Characteristics of Blood Flow

As blood moves through the heart with the various phases of the cardiac cycle, jets are created that have a given direction. In normal flow, the direction is always forward as the blood flows sequentially through the right atrium, then across the tricuspid valve into the right ventricle in diastole, then through the pulmonic valve into the pulmonary circulation in systole. Blood returning from the lungs then passes the left atrium, through the mitral valve into the left ventricle in diastole and then out across the aortic valve with ventricular systole. The movement of blood is driven by the sequential contractions of the cardiac chambers. As the chambers contract, high pressures are developed and blood flows from higher-pressure areas to lower-pressure areas.

With the sequential movements of the cardiac cycle, the blood is alternatively accelerated and decelerated with the pumping action of the heart. In normal blood flow, velocities are encountered that range from 0 m/sec, when the blood is not moving, to 1.5 m/sec as the left ventricle rapidly ejects the blood into the aorta.

In addition, all jets have certain sizes that relate roughly to their volume; if the volume is increased or decreased, the size of the jet is similarly increased or decreased.

The amount of blood ejected from a normal left ventricle in systole is approximately 100 ml. This is called stroke volume and is a common way to express volume flow.

Doppler Color Flow Imaging

Doppler color flow mapping, a new and exciting advance in cardiac ultrasound, is a method whereby blood flow is imaged and displayed on the two-dimensional echocardiographic image. Figure 1–1 shows a mitral regurgitant jet into the left atrium in systole. In color flow imaging, the colors red and blue represent direction of a given jet; the various hues from dull to bright represent the varying velocities. This results in a color map of a given jet with ready identification of size and direction. As a result, the Doppler information is given a spatial orientation that makes the flow information

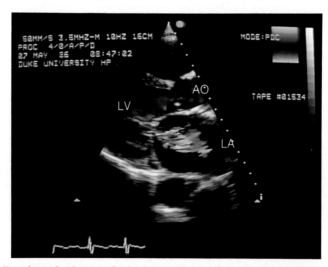

Fig. 1–1. Doppler color image of mitral regurgitation from the left parasternal long axis. Note the mitral valve closed in systole and the mitral regurgitant jet (in red) into the left atrium. LA = left atrium, Ao = aortic root, LV = left ventricle. For abbreviations used throughout this text see Appendix A.

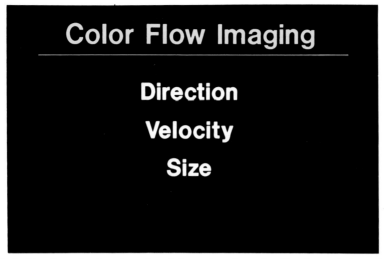

Fig. 1–2. Doppler color imaging gives information about the direction, relative velocity, and size of blood flow jets through the heart.

more readily understood when compared to conventional approaches.

The first step in understanding color flow is to realize that the characteristics of blood flow (direction, velocity, and size) (Fig. 1–2) are displayed onto the two-dimensional echocardiographic image by means of color encoding of the Doppler-generated flow signal. While the best way to visualize Doppler color flow information is in real time at the time of the examination, images may also be recorded on videotape for later playback and analysis. The color flow image shown in Figure 1–1 was photographed from a frozen image at the time of study and this format will be used throughout this book.

The Story of Doppler

The first description of the physical principles used in color flow devices is attributed to Johann Christian Doppler, an Austrian mathematician and scientist who lived in the first half of the nineteenth century. Doppler's first descriptions concerned changes in the wavelength of light as applied to astronomical events. In 1842, he presented a paper entitled "On the Coloured

Light of Double Stars and Some Other Heavenly Bodies," in which he postulated that certain properties of light emitted from stars depend upon the relative motion of the observer and the wave source. He suggested that the colored appearance of certain stars was caused by their motion relative to the earth, the blue ones moving toward earth and the red ones moving away.

He drew an analogy of a ship moving to meet, or retreat from, incoming ocean waves. The ship moving out to sea would meet the waves with more frequency than a ship moving toward the shoreline. Interestingly, Doppler never extrapolated his postulates to sound waves.

There was immediate criticism of Doppler. Just like today, critics abounded. Amongst them was Buys Ballot who in 1844 stated he simply did not believe Doppler. There is a rather amusing account of the difficulties Buys Ballot encountered in attempting to disclaim the Doppler effect. In 1845 he borrowed a steam locomotive from the Dutch government and arranged for a trumpet player to ride a flatcar as it approached and then left a station. Two other trumpet players were positioned on the ground, one to either

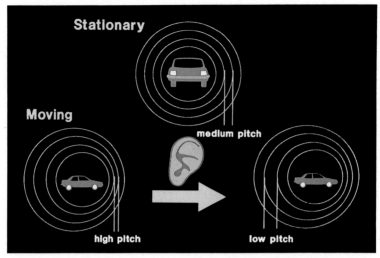

Fig. 1–3. Demonstration of emitted waves from stationary and moving objects. When stationary, the waves are equal in all directions. When moving toward an observer, the waves have a higher frequency than when moving away.

side, where an observer with the ability to appreciate perfect pitch listened to all the trumpets playing the same note. Following a hailstorm and other delays, the experiment finally took place. The note was higher in pitch as the train approached and lower in pitch as it departed when compared with the trumpets on the ground. Aside from verifying Doppler's observations, this experiment proved that "getting started in Doppler" was difficult even then.

Even with this scientific verification, Buys Ballot and others continued to level strong criticism. Those struggling to understand the Doppler principle will be interested to know that while Doppler's postulate concerning frequency shifts from moving objects was ultimately shown to be correct, his extrapolations about the color shift of light from stars was later proven to be wrong. He incorrectly assumed that all stars emitted white light. In reality, the colors and hues of the various stars are a function of their surface temperature rather than their direction or velocity of movement.

All readers of this volume are familiar with the Doppler effect in everyday life. For example, an observer stationed on a superhighway overpass easily notices that the pitch of the sound made from the engine of a passing automobile changes from high to low as the car approaches and then passes into the distance. The engine is emitting the same sound as it passes beneath, but the observer notices a change in pitch dependent upon the speed of the auto and its direction. Figure 1–3 demonstrates the changes in the frequency from an approaching and departing sound source in relation to a stationary sound source.

The Doppler effect is now employed in modern astronomy. It has practical applications in radar detection of storms and is used in modern weather forecasting. It even helps to form the "radar traps" used by police on modern highways to detect speeding automobiles.

The medical applications of Doppler are dependent upon the use of ultrasound and have been in practice for some time. Doppler systems emit a burst of very high-frequency sound, termed ultrasound, that is reflected off the moving red blood cells and then returned at a different frequency dependent upon the speed and direction of the moving blood. The resultant information is displayed as various waveforms on the velocity spectral analysis. The past five years have brought refinement in equipment and displays so that conventional pulsed and continuous-wave Doppler methods are now in widespread use throughout the world. Despite this widespread use, Doppler methods and principles are difficult to understand and implement without considerable training and experience. Details of the Doppler principle are described in Chapter 2.

The Importance of Color

The colors displayed on the flow map image contain useful information. Given two choices, red-toward with blue-away from the transducer or blue-toward with red-away from the transducer, most systems use the red-toward convention to display direction of flow. Therefore, most images displayed in this volume will be in this format.

This is in direct contrast to Doppler's original color assignments of the direction of moving stars. As best we can determine, the red-toward assignment was a modern development and was based upon Brandestini's color flow directional assignment in the early development of a carotid color flow scanner. With the transducer positioned on a carotid artery in these early studies, flow through the carotid was toward the transducer and encoded in red since hues of red are more readily recognized by the human eye. Venous flow in this orientation was away from the transducer and was encoded in blue.

Keeping arterial blood in red and venous blood in blue is both convenient and relatively easy when examining the carotid artery and jugular vein. In the heart, however, no such convenience is possible since valves and flows may be oriented in many different directions. Thus, the colors red and blue are indicators of direction and not oxygen content.

Doppler color flow systems assign a given color to the direction of flow. Two typical color bars from a color flow imaging device are shown in Figure 1–4 and given an initial frame of reference to the meaning of the colors. The center of the standard color bar at the left is

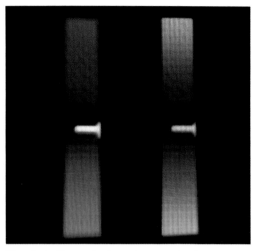

Fig. 1–4. Two color bars from a color flow system. When there is no flow, black is displayed (center line). In the standard bar at the left, flow toward the transducer at the top is in red, flow away in blue. Progressively faster velocities are displayed in brighter shades of red or blue. The colors have been enhanced in the bar at the right to help beginners understand the relative velocity information.

black (white center reference mark) and represents zero flow in the center. Red is generally represented as flow toward the transducer while blue is represented as flow away from the transducer. These color directional codes are presumably in honor of Doppler, despite his original error in color assignments. What results is that such color coding enables the user to easily obtain directional information.

In the color bar at the right, the colors have been "enhanced" so that the hues of red are increased from very dull red to bright yellow and the hues of blue are increased from very dull blue to a bright pale blue. The enhanced map helps a beginner to understand the meaning of color.

In addition to simple direction, velocity information is also displayed. Progressively increasing velocities are encoded in varying hues of either red or blue. The duller the hue, the slower the velocity. The brighter the hue, the faster the relative velocity. These bright colors are seen at the extremes of the representative color bars and more readily appreciated in the enhanced bar.

As will be seen later, color is also used to display turbulent flow and allows a user to discriminate between normal and abnormal flow states. The details of generation of the color-coded images are explained in Chapter 3.

The Angiographic Concept

All readers are readily familiar with angiographic concepts. The most familiar is cineangiography, in which a contrast material is injected into a cardiac chamber through a catheter and then visualized by radiographic methods. In this case, the x rays are the detectors of the injected contrast. Figure 1–5 shows a typical angiographic image from a left ventricle. In this method, the contrast material used is diluted within the left ventricle and outlines its borders. The resultant images are displayed as projected silhouettes.

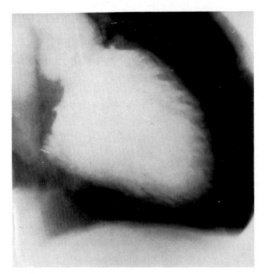

Fig. 1–5. Left ventricular cineangiogram in diastole obtained in the left anterior oblique position. The contrast is injected through a catheter and fills the ventricle. The image is a silhouette and obscures details of flow within the chamber due to superimposition.

Despite its widespread use, cineangiography has certain limitations. This approach almost always requires invasive cardiac catheterization as well as the use of ionizing radiation, both having attendant risks. While the resultant contrast silhouette has easily identifiable borders, information within the borders is obscured. Differential flows and anatomic targets within the borders are superimposed in the final image on top of one another.

One way of conceptualizing Doppler color flow methods is to recognize its similarity to angiography. It provides a noninvasive angiogram of blood flow where the contrast medium is the moving red blood cells and the detector of this contrast is ultrasound. The complex Doppler ultrasound processing circuitry allows for detection of movement of these red cells in various directions, forward and backward, through the heart. Doppler color flow information, however, is obtained and displayed in a cross-sectional image making the spatial details of flow and anatomy readily recognizable. In effect, Doppler color flow looks inside the cineangiographic silhouette.

The most readily understood application of these systems is in the detection of valvular regurgitation. Flow information is color-coded and superimposed on conventional two-dimensional echocardiographic images. The result is an easily appreciated representation of intracardiac flows and their relationships to one another and to anatomic structures. As in the case of mitral insufficiency, the direction of blood flow is abnormally reversed into the left atrium in systole. Doppler color flow systems are able to detect the abnormal direction of flow. Figure 1–6 shows two of many possible different directions of mitral regurgitation.

Unlike angiography, Doppler color flow does not depend upon dye dilution accumulated over several heartbeats. Rather, it displays an abnormal flow jet for *each* cardiac cycle. This results in the ability to display the differing sizes of regurgitant jets dependent upon severity. The larger the volume of the regurgitant jet, the larger the size represented on the display. Figure 1–7 uses the example of aortic insufficiency

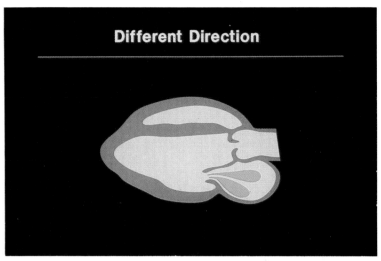

Fig. 1–6. Doppler color flow imaging can detect the different directions of abnormal jets. Here, two different mitral regurgitant jets are shown.

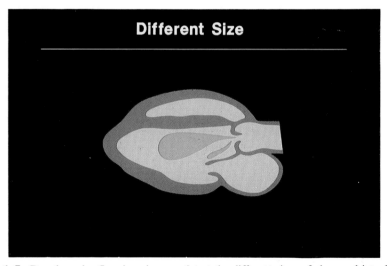

Fig. 1–7. Doppler color flow imaging can detect the different sizes of abnormal jets. Here, different sizes of aortic regurgitant jets are shown.

and shows two of many possible different sizes of regurgitant jets, one large and one small.

Thus, the potential clinical applications for Doppler color flow imaging are broad and include detection of valvular regurgitation, abnormal communications between cardiac chambers, flow through the great vessels, and the direction of stenotic jets. Despite the complexity of the electrical circuitry involved, the resultant images are relatively easy to interpret for users of two-dimensional echocardiography as the flow data is displayed on the moving image.

Relation of Color Flow to Other Methods

There are many other methods that are able to display blood flow through the heart. Radionuclide angiography also has common use but again requires ionizing radiation materials and lacks the spatial resolution usually found in ultrasonic approaches. Figure 1–8 shows a radionuclide angiogram from a patient with a pseudoaneurysm of the posterior wall of the left ventricle.

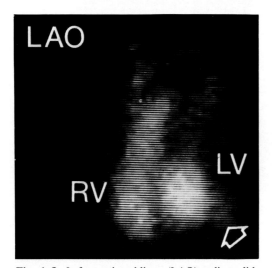

Fig. 1–8. Left anterior oblique (LAO) radionuclide image from a patient with a pseudoaneurysm of the left ventricle (arrow).

Real-time computed axial tomography systems (CT scanners) and magnetic resonance imaging (MRI) devices also provide ways to visualize blood flow. Figure 1–9 shows an MRI angiogram from a patient with aortic insufficiency. Both radionuclide and MRI imaging, however, require very expensive equipment costing roughly 10 to 15 times the cost of a color flow device. In addition, the cumbersome nature of the equipment precludes its use for examination of very sick patients where immediate results are required and transportation of the patient to the scanning device is difficult.

Color flow, however, has the advantages of being noninvasive, relatively inexpensive, readily portable, and possesses little patient risk in comparison to these other methods. The disadvantages of the method will become apparent in later discussions in this volume.

As a consequence, color flow methods are finding a unique role in cardiac diagnosis. In large institutions where all of the above imaging modalities are available these advantages are readily apparent. In small or medium-sized hospitals (or physicians' clinics and offices), where none of the other techniques are available, color flow approaches may assume a major role. In these settings, Doppler color flow mapping brings flow information into ready use for patient care. In our opinion, it can be conjectured that color flow methods, properly implemented in these settings, will save many unnecessary patient referrals and result in abundant savings to patients.

Relation to Conventional Doppler Methods

Conventional pulsed and continuous-wave Doppler methods are rapidly finding widespread applications worldwide. It is quite easy for a beginner to incorrectly assume that, since color flow approaches are the most recent, they must represent the most difficult and technically advanced methods for evaluation of heart disease using Doppler principles. Thus, before integrat-

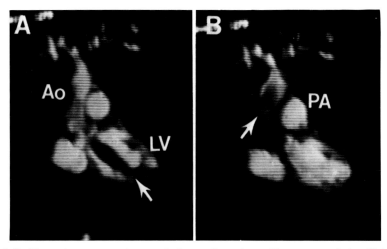

Fig. 1–9. Magnetic resonance image of a heart of a patient with severe aortic insufficiency. **(A)** Jet of aortic regurgitation in diastrole reaching the left venticular apex (arrow). **(B)** Blood flow filling the aortic root in systole (arrow). (Photo courtesy of Charles Spritzer, M.D. and Robert Herfkens, M.D., Duke University Medical Center.)

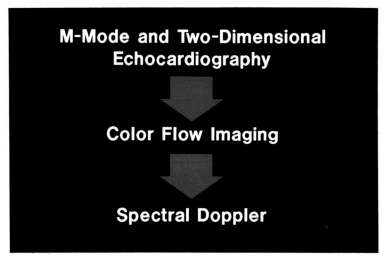

Fig. 1–10. Doppler color flow imaging reveals spatial information that is readily understood and may be used to guide the conventional Doppler examination.

ing color flow into clinical practice an operator must first master conventional methods.

In reality, however, the color flow display makes the Doppler data more readily understood because of the avoidance of complex spectral velocity displays. As a consequence, our continuing opinion is that color flow imaging in common clinical evaluation of patients has a role prior to the implementation of conventional methods in most cases (Fig. 1–10). Indeed, some users find beginning with the color flow a more readily understood and easily mastered method of implementing Doppler technology into their laboratories. All of these interrelationships will be discussed in Chapters 2 through 5.

Naming the Technique

Considerable argument still exists as to what to call any of these approaches. There are those who argue that the term "Doppler" should not be used for any of the pulsed approaches and that "frequency encoded M-mode" is more applicable. There are those who argue that the use of "color flow Doppler" is incorrect since motion, rather than flow, is displayed. Terms proposed for this technique include: "color motion," "color-coded Doppler flow mapping," "real-time Doppler color flow mapping," "Doppler color flow mapping," "color Doppler," "real-time two-dimensional Doppler flow imaging," "color flow imaging," and "color velocity imaging."

It is not our purpose to recommend any specific name nor enter into any argument concerning nomenclature. Rather, we trust the reader will understand that all of these terms refer basically to the same technique. As a consequence "color flow imaging" will be used most commonly.

References

1. Omoto R: Color Atlas of Real-Time Two-Dimensional Doppler Echocardiography. Shindan-To-Chiryo Co. Ltd. Tokyo, 1984
2. Kisslo J, Adams D, Mark DB: Basic Doppler Echocardiography. Churchill Livingstone, New York, 1986
3. Hatle L, Angelsen B: Doppler Ultrasound in Cardiology. 2nd Edition. Lea & Febiger, Philadelphia, 1985

2

Doppler Ultrasound and the Study of Cardiac Flow

It is possible, without being intimidated, to understand the very important principles of how Doppler systems work. This chapter presents the basic methods by which Doppler echocardiography may be used to study cardiac flow in a simple and logical sequence. Material covered serves as the fundamental building block to understand the color flow approach. It assumes no previous knowledge of Doppler methods and is a good place for readers untutored in Doppler to comfortably begin. Experienced and knowledgable users may wish to rapidly review these principles and move on to Chapter 3.

Detection of Flow Using Doppler

Unfortunately, the first place to start is with an equation. This equation helps the policeman with a radar gun determine how fast your automobile is traveling. In order to accomplish this feat, he aims the radar beam toward the highway at a given angle to intercept oncoming traffic. The device then sends out a radar beam of a given frequency which is then reflected from your moving oncoming automobile to the radar system at a higher frequency. The faster your automobile is traveling, the higher the returned frequency. The system is automatically programmed to know the fixed speed of the radar

beam in air. All these factors are then placed into our equation to determine whether you receive a speeding ticket.

What was learned about the Doppler effect in the previous chapter can be expressed as an equation that has very important implications in performing and interpreting Doppler echocardiographic examinations. Understanding this equation will certainly aid any reader in perfecting his or her Doppler skills and may even aid in arguing with the policeman mentioned above.

Simply stated, the Doppler shift (F_d) of ultrasound will depend on both the transmitted frequency (f_0) and the velocity (V) of the moving blood (Fig. 2–1). This returned frequency is also called the "frequency shift" or "Doppler shift" and is highly dependent upon the angle (cos θ) between the beam of ultrasound transmitted from the transducer and the moving red blood cells. The velocity of sound in blood is constant (c) and is an important part of the Doppler equation.

The most accurate frequency shift is detected when the ultrasound beam is parallel to flow. As the angle between beam and flow becomes larger, the less reliable is the frequency shift. This has very important implications for Doppler echocardiography since it requires the operator to direct the beam as nearly parallel to flow as possible for the most accurate Doppler results.

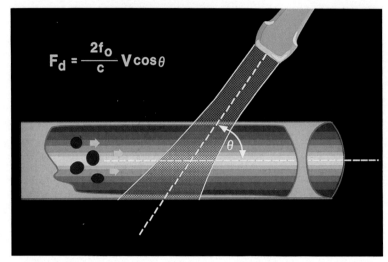

Fig. 2–1. The Doppler equation. As red blood cells move through a vessel they intercept a Doppler beam at a given angle θ. (After materials from the Irex Corporation.)

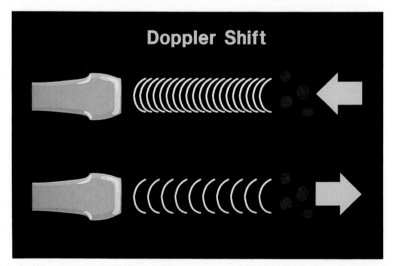

Fig. 2–2. The Doppler shift. Red cells moving toward the transducer would result in a shift to a frequency higher than transmitted. As they move away, a shift to a lower frequency than transmitted results. (After materials from the Irex Corporation.)

Knowledge of the various relationships found in the basic Doppler equation is important to establish a further understanding of the technique. The reader should realize, however, that all these various complex mathematical calculations are performed within any Doppler instrument in an automated way.

Direction of Blood Flow

The ability to detect frequency shifts from moving red cells forms the basis by which Doppler systems identify direction of movement. As applied to Doppler ultrasound, the frequency shift detected from red cells approaching the transducer will be higher than the transmitted frequency (Fig. 2–2) and is termed a "positive Doppler shift." Alternatively, the frequency shift detected from red cells moving away from the transducer will be lower than the transmitted frequency and is termed a "negative Doppler shift."

Automated circuits within any Doppler instrument are able to compare the transmitted frequency to the returned frequency and calculate the various frequency shifts. Since actual frequencies are compared (transmitted to returned) within the instrument, "phase shifts" are determined (Fig. 2–3). Red cells moving away from the transducer will result in a returned frequency lower than transmitted and give a negative phase shift ($-\Delta P$). Red cells moving toward the transducer will result in a returned frequency higher than transmitted and give a positive phase shift ($+\Delta P$).

Velocity of Blood Flow

A simple rearrangement of the Doppler equation allows for measurement of actual velocities of the moving red cells (Fig. 2–4). For cardiac Doppler, all hard-copy outputs are expressed in velocity shifts rather than frequency shifts by convention. Again, the calculation of blood flow velocity takes place within the Doppler ultrasound system.

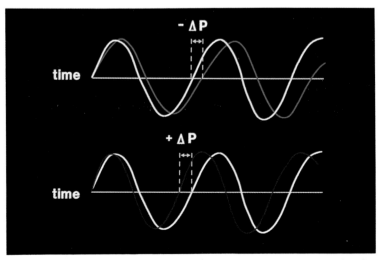

Fig. 2–3. Diagram of a reference transmitted wave in white. Since the returning frequency from red cells moving away from the transducer is lower than transmitted (blue wave), a negative phase shift occurs; since the returning frequency from red cells moving toward the transducer is higher than transmitted (red wave), a positive phase shift occurs.

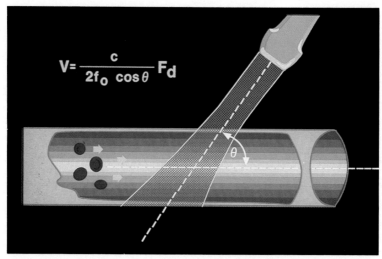

Fig. 2–4. The Doppler equation rearranged to solve for velocity. (After materials from the Irex Corporation.)

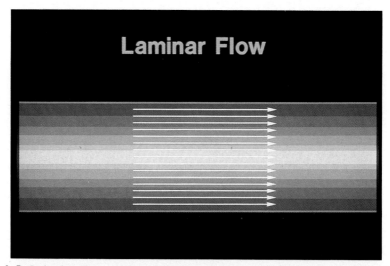

Fig. 2–5. In laminar flow, all the red cells are moving at approximately the same velocity and direction. In reality, the velocity of flow just adjacent to the vessel walls is slightly slower than at the center. (After materials from the Irex Corporation.)

As previously mentioned, it is very important to know that the Doppler beam is as parallel to flow as possible for the most reliable recording of velocity. The angle θ (between the ultrasound beam and the direction of the moving red cells) will determine the magnitude of the calculated velocity. If the ultrasound beam is parallel to flow, cosine $\theta = 1$, then the measured Doppler shift will represent the true velocity of the red cell. As θ varies from $0°$, the detected Doppler shift will increasingly underestimate the true velocity. What results in such a case is not the true velocity of the moving red cells but something *less*. If θ becomes too

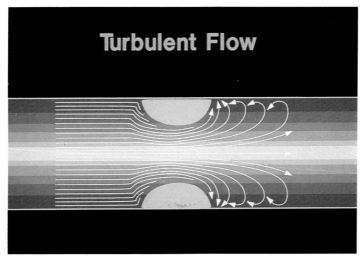

Fig. 2–6. In turbulent flow, the red cells have many different velocities and directions, in this case because of an obstruction. (After materials from the Irex Corporation.)

large, the represented velocity differs significantly from the true velocity. In fact, if the beam is 60° from parallel, the calculated value will be approximately one-half of true velocity!

Estimations of true velocity have variable importance in Doppler echocardiography. As will be seen later, if an operator simply wants to locate an area of turbulence, the angle of approach may have little importance. If, however, measurement of peak velocity is required, it is absolutely essential that the beam be as parallel to flow as possible.

Laminar and Turbulent Flows

In addition to direction and velocity, blood flow through the heart and great vessels may be laminar (normal) or turbulent (disturbed). Laminar flow is flow that occurs along smooth parallel lines in a vessel or through a valve when all the red cells in an area are moving at approximately the same speed and in the same direction (Fig. 2–5). In laminar flow, the velocity adjacent to the walls of a vessel is really slightly less than that in the center. This figure has been prepared with all the arrows of equal length for the sake of simplicity. With the pulsa-

tions of the heart, the red cells generally accelerate and decelerate at approximately the same speed. Flow in most of the cardiovascular system, including the heart and great vessels, is normally laminar. Normal blood flow through the heart rarely exceeds 1.5 m/sec.

In contrast, turbulent or disturbed flow is said to be present when there is some obstruction that results in a disruption of the normal laminar pattern (Fig. 2–6). This causes the orderly movement of red blood cells to become disorganized and produces various whorls and eddies of differing velocities and directions. Obstruction to flow usually also results in some increase in velocity. Thus, turbulent flow is characterized by disordered directions of flow in combination with many different red cell velocities. If the obstruction is significant, some of the red blood cells may be moving at higher velocities than normal and may reach speeds of 5 or 6 m/sec. Turbulent flow is usually an abnormal finding and is considered indicative of some underlying cardiovascular pathology.

Conventional Doppler Displays

Some understanding of how conventional Doppler displays are presented is necessary to properly understand the differences among these approaches and those used in color flow methods. All conventional pulsed and continuous-wave Doppler systems provide an audio output of the various frequency shifts encountered. Velocities detected by the Doppler instrument are converted into audible sounds emitted from speakers within the machine. High-pitched sounds result from large Doppler shifts and indicate the presence of high velocities, while low-pitched sounds result from lesser Doppler shifts and lower velocities. Laminar flow produces a smooth, pleasant tone, while turbulent flow results in a high-pitched and whistling sound or a harsh and raspy sound. Audio output is useful in the conduct of the Doppler examination because it aids the sonographer in achieving proper orientation of the ultrasound beam with respect to the flow area of interest.

Data from conventional pulsed and continuous-wave systems are generally displayed visually in the form of a hard-copy velocity spectrum. The velocity spectra are derived from computer-facilitated frequency analysis of the reflected ultrasound signal. Such an analysis is accomplished within the Doppler machine using digital methods (most commonly with the Fast Fourier Transform method) or analog methods (the Chirp-Z Transform method). Both methods are simply electronic ways of handling vast amounts of confusing data in a very short period of time. In this way Doppler frequency shifts from multiple moving red cells, often with disparate velocities, can be processed and displayed.

The construction of velocity spectra may be easily understood without a detailed knowledge of the processing methods employed. Figure 2–7 shows a schematic diagram of a velocity spectral analysis using the concept of displaying the velocity data into various bins. As the Doppler instrument receives the various frequency shifts from the moving red cells the data are presented to the spectrum analyzer where the differing velocities are prepared for display. The spectral recording can be imagined to be made up of a series of "bins" (vertical axis) that are recorded over time (horizontal axis). As flow accelerates and decelerates the various velocities are displayed on the spectral recording.

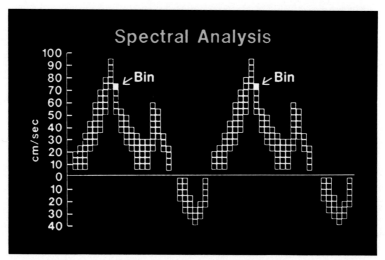

Fig. 2–7. Conventional Doppler flow velocity data are displayed as a spectrum of velocities present at any time. Thus, relative velocities toward and away from the transducer are displayed above or below the baseline into bins of information. (After material from Hewlett-Packard, Inc.)

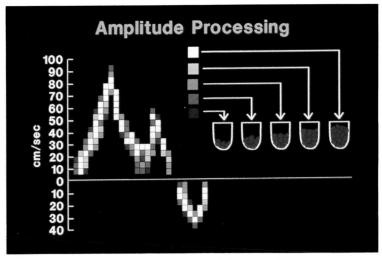

Fig. 2–8. Within the spectral velocity display, the brightness of any bin reflects the number of red blood cells traveling at that velocity. The brighter the bin, the more red cells present. (After material from Hewlett-Packard, Inc.)

Even in laminar flow, the moving red cells display somewhat different velocities at any instant. The more red cells that are moving with a particular velocity at a given time, the more intense will be the corresponding bin at that time (Fig. 2–8). Similarly, the fewer the red cells moving at any given velocity the less intense the resultant display. This spectral display is termed "amplitude processing" because the various amplitudes of intensity are presented in the display. The spectral display is thus a complex plot of the various velocities recorded over time (Fig. 2–9).

In spectral displays, when there is no flow there is no Doppler velocity shift. Flow toward the transducer is represented above the baseline while flow away from the transducer is represented below the baseline.

When normal laminar flow is encountered, the resultant spectral recording will be relatively smooth because all the red cells are moving in the same direction, accelerating and decelerating at nearly the same velocity. An example of this narrow spectrum of velocities when a Doppler beam is angled from the suprasternal notch into the ascending aorta in a normal individual is seen in Figure 2–10A. In contrast, when turbulent flow is encountered, the resulting velocity spectrum is broadened because there are many red cells moving at many different velocities. Turbulent flow from an aortic stenotic jet in the ascending aorta is seen in Figure 2–10B. Such turbulent flows are typically encountered in regurgitant or stenotic jets.

Conventional Pulsed and Continuous-Wave Doppler

To understand color flow methods, it is first essential to understand the operating characteristics of conventional systems. Continuous-wave Doppler is the older and electronically simpler of the two methods. Continuous-wave Doppler involves continuous transmission of ultrasound waves coupled with continuous ultrasound reception. This is accomplished with a two-crystal transducer. One crystal is devoted to each function (Fig. 2–11).

The continuous wave system is always transmitting and receiving (Fig. 2–12A). The main advantage of continuous-wave Doppler is its

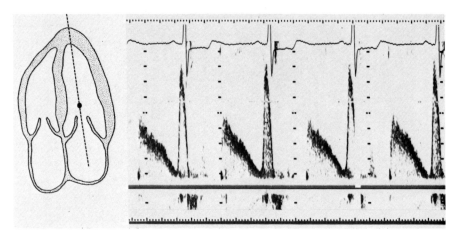

Fig. 2–9. Conventional pulsed Doppler spectral analysis recording of flow with the sample volume located at the mitral orifice. Laminar mitral diastolic flow is seen toward the transducer and no spectral broadening is present. When the background is white, the darker the data at any bin the higher the number of red cells at that velocity. (Adams D, Mark DB, Kisslo J: The Doppler examination. p. 63. In Kisslo J, Adams D, Mark DB (eds): Basic Doppler Echocardiography. Churchill Livingstone, New York, 1986).

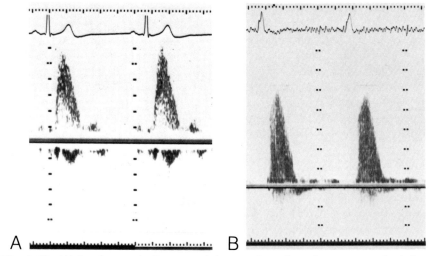

Fig. 2–10. (A) Laminar aortic flow toward the transducer from the suprasternal window. All the red cells are accelerating and decelerating at approximately the same velocity, resulting in a relatively clean spectral recording. Each single dot on the scale is 20 cm/sec. **(B)** Spectral recording of turbulent aortic stenotic flow where many velocities are present at any one time and peak velocity is elevated. The double dot scale marks represent 1 m/sec.

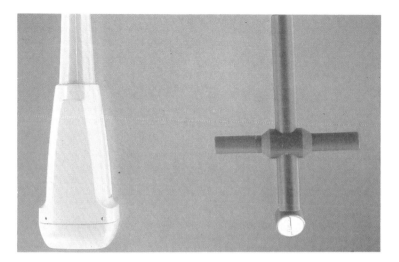

Fig. 2–11. Hand-held transducers used in Doppler echocardiography. A continuous-wave transducer is at left. Notice the double sided face allowing for separate simultaneous transmission and reception. A two-dimensional echocardiographic transducer is at the right; conventional pulsed Doppler is most commonly carried out with this type of transducer.

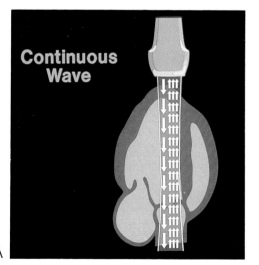

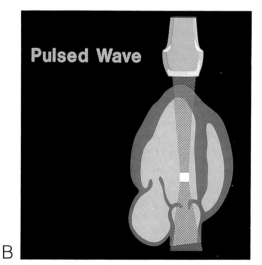

A   B

Fig. 2–12. (A) Continuous-wave Doppler beam with constant, and independent, transmission and reception. **(B)** Pulsed wave beam, where transmission is to and from a single point within the beam.

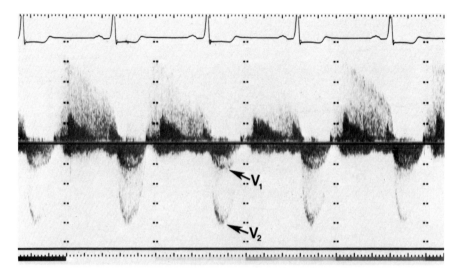

Fig. 2–13. Spectral velocity recording from a continuous-wave Doppler beam angled from the apex toward the left ventricular outflow tract in a patient with combined aortic stenosis and insufficiency. Turbulent flow above the baseline throughout diastole results from aortic insufficiency. Turbulent flow below the baseline is across the aortic valve in systole. V_1 is the velocity on the ventricular side of the aortic valve. V_2 is the elevated velocity on the distal side of the valve that results from the stenosis and approaches 4 m/sec. Scale marks represent 1 m/sec. (Kisslo J, Krafchek J, Adams D, Mark DB: Doppler evaluation of valvular stenosis. p. 123. In Kisslo J, Adams D, Mark DB (eds): Basic Doppler Echocardiography. Churchill Livingstone, New York, 1986.)

ability to accurately measure high blood cell velocities. Indeed, continuous-wave Doppler can accurately record the highest velocities encountered in any valvular or congenital heart disease. Figure 2–13 demonstrates a diastolic velocity spectrum from aortic insufficiency toward the transducer and a high velocity systolic jet of aortic stenosis away from the transducer. Determination of maximal velocity is important in the quantitative assessment of certain valvular disorders.

The main disadvantage of continuous wave is its lack of depth discrimination. Since it is constantly transmitting and receiving from two different crystals, there is no time left over to create a two-dimensional image. Nor is there the possibility to time gate transmission and reception in order to provide depth information. The output from a continuous-wave examination contains Doppler shift data from every reflecting red cell along the course of the ultrasound beam.

Since true continuous-wave Doppler requires continuous transmission and reception, no time is available for creation of the two-dimensional image. The absence of anatomic information during a continuous-wave examination may lead to interpretive difficulties, particularly if more than one heart chamber or blood vessel lies in the path of the Doppler beam. As a result, some newer ultrasound systems incorporate the continuous-wave capability into the two-dimensional system to allow guidance of the beam as well as switching back and forth between imaging and continuous-wave interrogations.

Practically speaking, continuous-wave interrogation methods cannot be readily incorporated into color flow systems. No range information is available to place the flow velocity data easily on the moving two-dimensional display. On the other hand, Doppler color flow mapping is a sophisticated extension of the pulsed Doppler principle. Pulsed-wave Doppler uses a transducer which alternately transmits and receives ultrasound information and may readily be incorporated using the same two-dimensional transducer (Fig. 2–11).

One main advantage of pulsed Doppler is its ability to provide Doppler shift data selectively from a small region along the ultrasound beam (Fig. 2–12B). This region is referred to as the sample volume. The location of the sample volume is operator-controlled. An ultrasound pulse is transmitted into the tissues, travels for a given time (time X) until it encounters the moving red cells at that location, and then returns to the transducer over the same time interval. The total transit time to and from the area sampled is $2X$. Since the speed of ultrasound in tissue is constant, and the time of transit is known, the distance between the reflecting red cell and the transducer can be easily calculated. This process is alternately and rapidly repeated through many transmit–receive cycles.

The ability to identify the point in space from which reflected ultrasound originates is known as "range gating." If the operator chooses a particular location for the sample volume, the range gate circuit will permit only Doppler shift data from inside that area to be displayed. Other returning ultrasound information is essentially "ignored."

Another advantage of pulsed Doppler is the fact that some imaging may be carried on alternatively with the Doppler, and the sample volume may be shown on the actual two-dimensional display for guidance (Fig. 2–14). When pulsed Doppler is conducted with the two-dimensional image for guidance the Doppler and the imaging cannot be conducted at the same time. In these systems, the Doppler data are collected and then the two-dimensional image is intermittently updated. Pulsed-wave Doppler

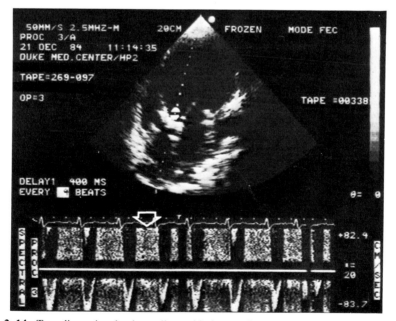

Fig. 2–14. Two-dimensional echocardiographic image showing the sample volume located just below the aortic valve in the apical four-chamber view (above). The spectral recording below shows the velocity "cut off" and placed into the opposite channel below in diastole (arrow).

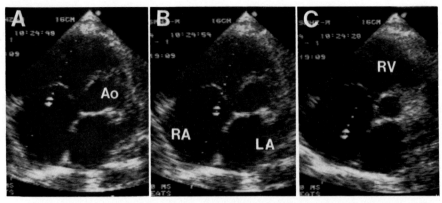

Fig. 2–15. Successive two-dimensional echocardiographic images from the parasternal short axis showing different sample volume placements used for locating turbulence in different spatial locations. (Mark DB, Robertson JH, Adams D, Kisslo J: Doppler evaluation of valvular regurgitation. p. 91. In Kisslo J, Adams D, Mark DB (eds): Basic Doppler Echocardiography. Churchill Livingstone, New York, 1986.)

capability is possible in combination with imaging from a mechanical or phased-array imaging system. It is also generally steerable by the operator through the two-dimensional field of view (Fig. 2–15).

The major disadvantage of pulsed Doppler is that it is constrained by the time necessary for the interrogating pulse to reach the area of interest and then return. Practically this results in a phenomenon known as "aliasing," where the velocity of rapidly moving red cells exceeds the ability of the pulsed Doppler system to accurately record their speed. Table 2–1 compares the advantages and limitations of conventional Doppler approaches.

The best Doppler data are collected when parallel to flow and this orientation requirement usually results in imaging planes where the in-terrogating beam is also parallel to the anatomic targets. Thus, it is not common to have ideal two-dimensional images and ideal Doppler data simultaneously.

Aliasing

The phenomenon of aliasing is best explained using a simple example (Fig. 2–16). A red mark is placed on a turning wheel, and the wheel rotates in a clockwise direction at a speed of one turn every four seconds. If the sampling rate (or pulse repetition frequency) is one sample per second, the mark is recorded at each progressive 90-degree position. The final recording would then show the proper clockwise direction of motion of the wheel (left column).

If the sampling rate (or pulse repetition frequency) is slowed to only one sample every three seconds, the phenomenon of aliasing occurs (right column). Note that the mark is moving 270 degrees between sampling times, and that while actually turning clockwise the recording makes the wheel appear to be moving in the opposite, or counterclockwise, direction.

Table 2–1. Comparison of Conventional Doppler Techniques

	Range Resolution	Limitation on Maximum Velocity
Pulsed wave	Yes	Yes
Continuous wave	No	No

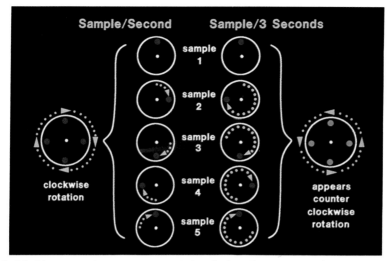

Fig. 2–16. Diagrammatic representation of the aliasing phenomenon. For details, see text.

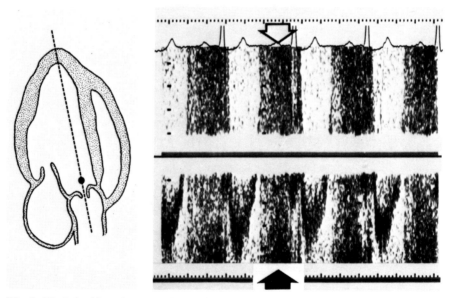

Fig. 2–17. Pulsed Doppler spectral recording of aliasing of aortic insufficiency. Flow toward the transducer (open arrow) is "cut off" and placed at the bottom of the record (closed arrow). The diagram at left shows the location of the sample volume just below the aortic valve. (Mark DB, Robertson JH, Adams D, Kisslo J: Doppler evaluation of valvular regurgitation. p. 91. In Kisslo J, Adams D, Mark DB (eds): Basic Doppler Echocardiography. Churchill Livingstone, New York, 1986.)

This also the reason why propellers and wagon wheels appear to go backward on movie film since the film frame rate is too slow to accurately keep up with these rapidly moving structures. A blue dot has been placed on the resultant image of the turning wheel in this illustration. As will be seen later, aliasing is represented in the color flow image as a reversal in color.

When this occurs in pulsed Doppler echocardiography, the velocity reaches a point where it exceeds the ability of the system to keep up and the velocity is "cut off" (ambiguous) and placed into the opposite channel (Fig. 2–17). It appears as a reversal of flow when none has occurred in reality. In practical terms this results in an inability of pulsed Doppler to faithfully record velocities above 1.5 to 2 m sec when the sample volume is located at standard depths within the heart.

In many disease states, such as valvular regurgitation and stenosis, the velocities of flow are high and exceed 2 or 3 m/sec. This commonly results in the aliasing phenomenon when using pulsed Doppler approaches. Since color flow Doppler uses pulsed techniques, such aliasing has a profound effect on the use and interpretation of color flow imaging data.

Nyquist Limit

The Nyquist limit defines when aliasing will occur using pulsed-wave Doppler and may be expressed as:

$$\text{Nyquist limit} = \frac{\text{number pulses/second}}{2}$$

The Nyquist limit specifies that measurements of velocity are accurate (unambiguous) only if the pulse repetition frequency (PRF) is at least twice the maximum velocity encountered in the sample volume.

The closer the sample volume is located from the transducer, the higher the maximum PRF that can be used. Conversely, the farther the sample volume is located to the transducer, the lower the maximum PRF becomes. This is true because the distance (and therefore pulse travel time) to and from the sample volume is much shorter in the near field and, therefore, pulse round-trip transit time is much less when compared with greater distances. Thus, for any given high velocity jet, if it is located in the far field of the image, aliasing will occur. If it happens to be in the near field, somewhere close to the transducer face, it might be that no aliasing occurs.

Color Flow Imaging

Color flow imaging requires that the ultrasound system work very quickly to create the two-dimensional image and almost simultaneously acquire the Doppler information throughout the field of view. Color flow mapping uses an extension of pulsed Doppler range gating techniques as shall be seen in Chapter 3.

3

Creation of the Color Image

In order to maximize the use of any color imaging system it is necessary to understand its operation. All systems are digitally based, which simply means that the complex flow datum is assigned a given number. In some ways, therefore, the creation of the color flow Doppler may be likened to an electronic "paint by number" landscape scene. The key to color flow is to understand how the color flow system determines the number to be painted in each area of the landscape. In this chapter we attempt to unravel the mysteries and complexities of how the two-dimensional color flow Doppler image is created.

The Importance of Time

Time is the key factor to keep in mind. A conventional two-dimensional ultrasound imaging system is already working as hard as it can. Pulses must be transmitted along a given line, reflected from the heart valves and walls, then received. The process is then repeated, line by line, through the entire sector arc that is comprised of several hundred lines. This completes one frame of information, usually in one-30th of a second. In order to have the image appear as though it is continuously moving, the entire image must be updated again and again every one-30th of a second (30 frames/sec). This results in relatively very long waiting periods for

the transmit–receive sequence to be completed. It also results in tremendous amounts of information to be quickly processed and presented in the image.

A problem, therefore, results. If all this time is taken up in simply creating the image, where is there time left over to rapidly sample the Doppler, left and right, in all portions of the image field? From Chapter 2 we have already learned that high-quality imaging and high-quality pulsed Doppler cannot really be conducted simultaneously.

Anatomic and Flow Information Together

Expressed in its most simplistic terms, color flow systems add a separate processor that creates the color flow image based upon the returning data and then integrates it with the two-dimensional anatomic image (Fig. 3–1). Both the anatomic and the color flow data are then displayed in the final image.

The returning ultrasound data from any conventional scanner also contain frequency shift information that results from the encounter of the transmitted pulse with moving structures and blood. Until the advent of color flow imaging, these frequency shift data were simply ignored.

The key to color flow mapping is found in

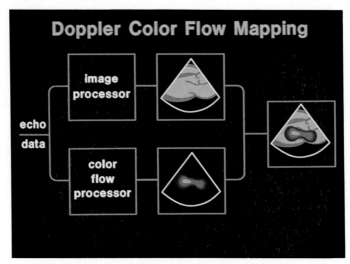

Fig. 3–1. In a color flow imaging device the returning echo data are processed through two channels that ultimately combine the image with the color flow data in the final display.

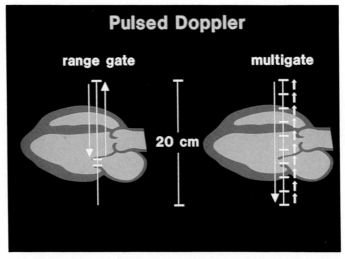

Fig. 3–2. Color flow Doppler systems are pulsed Doppler principles in a multigate, rather than range gate, format. For details, see text.

the fact that the returning data may also be processed for the frequency shifts (or red blood cell velocities). Thus, color flow imaging systems take advantage of data that are available in every ultrasound image of the heart.

While this is a very simplistic explanation, it is not true in most color flow systems. In reality, the lines of color flow data are alternated with lines of anatomic scan data. The anatomic data is acquired and received by conventional means and the color flow data are acquired, received, and processed by the methods explained in the remaining sections of this chapter.

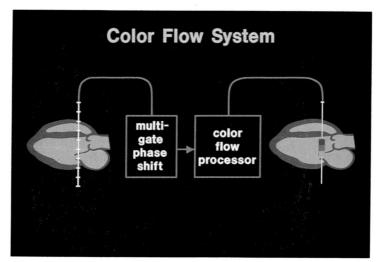

Fig. 3–3. Color flow imaging systems collect the phase shift information at each of the multiple gates and then process the information with color presented in the final diplay.

Multigate Doppler

Doppler color flow instruments are all currently based upon pulsed Doppler methods. Simple conventional pulsed techniques are range gated (Fig. 3–2, left). The Doppler sample volume is determined in range by the time it takes for the ultrasound pulse to travel to the area of interest and then back. If the same method were employed in color flow it would simply take too long to sample over the entire image and there would be serious compromises made in frame rate.

Rather, all color flow systems are "multigated." In the illustration in the right-hand panel of Fig. 3–2 a simple 10-gate system is illustrated and compared with the conventional pulsed approach. Here, a burst of ultrasound is sent into the tissue along a given line and then the system rapidly receives at 10 incremental times. This results in the reception of Doppler data from the near flow areas first while he pulse is still continuing into the tissue. Obviously, reception of the flow data in the far field occurs later.

This multigating takes advantage of Doppler information all along the line that is "ignored" in the conventional range gated approach. In reality, each line has many gates that number in the hundreds. Figure 3–3 demonstrates a simple 10-gate system where the amplitude and phase shifts are detected for each gate and present to the color flow processor for final display of the color in each gate.

It is good to think of the flow map image as comprised of little gates throughout the field of view, each gate containing some composite of the Doppler information. A typical image may be comprised of as many as 256 lines depending upon sector size and depth of range. Figure 3–4 demonstrates that multiple gates of color flow information are displayed throughout the entire image along each ultrasound line.

About the Meaning of Color

All Doppler flow imaging systems encode the direction of flow into two primary colors, red and blue. Any number of color assignments could be made but red and blue are chosen because they are primary colors of light (along with green). Most color flow systems now display the direction of flow toward the transducer in red and away from the transducer in blue.

There is also relative flow velocity informa-

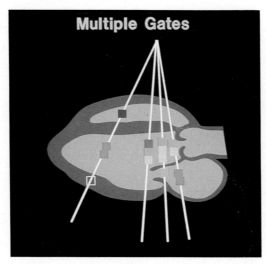

Fig. 3–4. Hundreds of gates are present along each line everywhere in the color flow image. In gates where there is target information, no color is displayed (open gate at lower left).

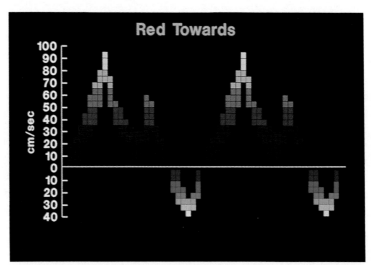

Fig. 3–5. If color were mapped on a conventional spectral recording only one color could be placed in each bin. Progressively increasing velocities toward the transducer would be displayed in brighter hues of red while flow away would be displayed in blue.

tion in the color hues; the brighter the color, the higher the velocity detected. Thus, high velocities away from the transducer will appear as lighter shades of blue (using the standard "blue-away" format), and higher velocities toward the transducer will be represented by lighter shades of red or even yellow. Low-velocity flow will be represented by darker shades

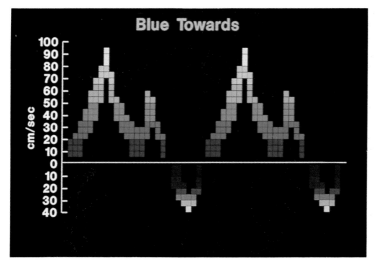

Fig. 3–6. Colors could also be reversed with progressively increasing velocities toward the transducer displayed in brighter hues of blue while flow away is displayed in red.

of these colors. No flow is always represented by black. If such encoding were done on a conventional spectral Doppler display the result would look very much like Figure 3–5. Color assignments are totally arbitrary, however, and the opposite assignments could also be used and are shown in Figure 3–6 where the "blue-toward" standard is used.

Figure 3–7 compares the identical images of mitral regurgitation, one in the "red-toward" (Fig. 3–7A) and the other in the "blue-toward" format (Fig. 3–7B).

Choosing a Velocity for Display

Careful study of Figure 3–8 should reveal a problem for the color flow map display. Even in laminar flow, many different velocities (and therefore colors) may be detected at any instant in time. In the two-dimensional display, only one color can be displayed in each gate at any time. The problem is even worse when turbulent flows are detected where there may be a wide range of velocities at any instant. At each spatial location, or gate, only one color is to be displayed for any selected map. What color should be chosen?

Detection of Mean Velocity

The color presented at each gate is determined by the mean velocity at any instant in time. Mean velocity is the average of all the different velocities detected at any moment in time. For normal laminar flow, mean and peak velocity are very close (Fig. 3–8). In turbulent flow, when there are many different velocities mean velocity may be only half of the peak velocity.

Thus, for a flow map system to correctly assign a color into a given gate, it must be able to detect both the direction of flow and the mean velocity in the area sampled. Since everything must happen very quickly it is best to think of flow map systems as estimating, rather than precisely calculating, the mean velocity at any gate.

About Pulses, Packets, and Trains

The calculation of mean velocity presents an intriguing problem. If you were asked to determine the mean (average) height of a hundred people lined up before you, you would want to measure each individual, then divide by the

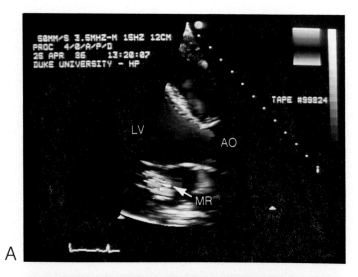

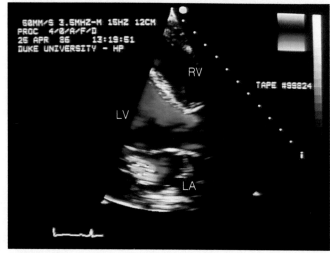

Fig. 3–7. (A) Red-toward map in the parasternal long axis from a patient with mitral insufficiency. The insufficiency jet aliases from red to blue. **(B)** Identical frame, except in the blue-toward map where the insufficiency jet aliases into red.

number of people measured and arrive at the true mean height. Such a procedure would take considerable time and considerable equipment and personnel.

If the time and equipment were not available, you might want to measure just one person at random and hope that your number reflected the entire population. But if you were given another brief period to measure another person, you would arrive at a better estimate because you could take the height from the first sample time and add it to the second sample time (then divide by 2). Given a third, fourth, and perhaps fifth sample period you would progressively arrive at a better estimate of mean height in the population. This is an imperfect way to estimate

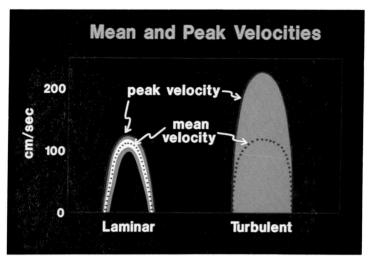

Fig. 3–8. Schematic representation of a spectral recording showing the differences between peak and mean velocities. In the case of normal laminar flow, peak and mean velocities may be very close. For turbulent flow, there may be a significant difference between peak and mean velocity.

mean height; under the limitation of time and equipment it is, however, the only way.

The problem is similar for the flow map device. Since there are very narrow time constraints for the system to do all of its estimations of mean velocity at any gate, then process the results for presentation, ways need to be devised to get the best estimates possible and then move on. Naturally, compromises must be made along the way.

Color flow systems use an elaborate sequence of pulses to arrive at these estimates; all are shown in Figure 3–9. The ultrasound transducer transmits sound waves at a given frequency (f) and the frequency is fixed by the transducer being used (2.5, 3.5, or 5.0 MHz). Bursts of pulses are known as the "pulse train." The time between successive pulse trains determines the pulse repetition frequency (PRF). A number of pulse trains are also emitted at a given angle and this is called the "packet size." In color flow mapping the principle of packet size is particularly important as it determines the length of time for sampling to occur before the system moves on to the next beam line.

For conventional two-dimensional anatomic imaging, only a single pulse train is used to acquire the necessary anatomic information. In these cases, relatively great time is available because no complex frequency analysis needs to be performed.

In conventional pulsed Doppler typically 128 pulse trains are required to obtain detailed velocity spectra from a single point in space. Since the sample volume is held in one place there is plenty of time to perform the detailed spectral analysis. Because color flow mapping attempts to estimate velocity at multiple points in space, far fewer pulse trains can be employed. Time will simply not permit such detailed sampling and the construction of a two-dimensional flow image simultaneously.

Color flow requires the most samples possible in the shortest period of time because so much Doppler data need to be acquired. The pulse packet length is directly analogous to the 128 pulse trains in conventional pulsed Doppler. However, the packet length is considerably less than 128. The more pulse trains in a given packet, the better the resulting estimates of

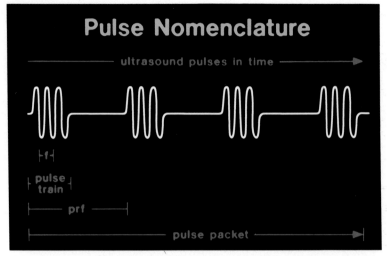

Fig. 3–9. Pulse nomenclature used in the development of color flow images. It is the number of pulse trains that determine the size of the pulse packet. The larger the packet the better the estimation of mean flow velocity. Abbreviations: f = frequency; prf = pulse repetition frequency.

mean velocity. At least three pulse trains per line (or a packet size 3) are required, and up to 16 pulse trains (or a packet size 16) may be used. Obviously, large packet sizes give the best estimates of flow but require the longest time.

Clinical Implications of Packet Size

The requirement for multiple pulse trains per line means that a greater period of time is required to sample along each beam direction than in conventional two-dimensional imaging. Thus, some reduction in frame rate, line density, or sector angle in comparison to routine two-dimensional imaging study is necessary. When turned into the color flow mode an operator will immediately notice compromises made in these factors.

Sector angle and depth range can be chosen. In some systems packet size can also be selected. Once these factors are determined, frame rate and line density are automatically adjusted according to the specifications of the

particular system (although in some systems line density can also be selected by the operator). In general, better quality flow data will be obtained with a higher packet size since this allows more sampling along each beam direction. Choosing a higher packet size, however, necessitates either a smaller line density or a lower frame rate and will affect the quality of the image in other ways to be discussed later.

Color Processing

The next step is to understand a bit of how these systems process the returning wave forms and assign a given color. Reflected ultrasound from tissue is processed and displayed conventionally, leading to the creation of a tomographic two-dimensional image as seen in Figure 3–1.

The analysis of returning Doppler signals from each sector line is complex. The frequency shift (or Doppler shift) between transmitted ultrasound and returning ultrasound can be processed as in conventional pulsed Doppler, with a circuit called the "quadrature detector." This device employs common electronic circuits to allow determination of both the magnitude and direction of the frequency shifts. Simply understood, the quadrature detector supplies a measurement to be used later for the color flow processor in assigning the velocity, and thus the color, at any gate. The main function of the quadrature detector is to make this phase shift measurement for each pulse train, then convert it from analog to digital form (which simply means the data from a continuous sine wave form are assigned a given number to allow further high speed processing). This digital measurement is then sent to the color flow processor for assignment of velocity and then color.

To obtain the best estimates of flow possible, the signals must first be cleaned as the frequency shifts are cluttered by system noise and other signals that arise from heart valves and other structures. Returning data from one pulse train are held in the processor memory to be used for eliminating system noise from all the other pulse trains in the packet. Data from the second pulse train then return and are compared to the first leaving a single clean signal. The third pulse train then returns and is cleaned in a similar fashion. To get a single phase shift the two clean signals (second and third) are then compared. Thus, to get a single measurement of phase shift a minimum of three pulse trains is required. This filtering, or cleaning process, utilizes "clutter reject filters" or "comb filters."

Instead of determining the frequency shift at a single depth, as in conventional pulsed Doppler, frequency shifts are determined from multiple sample volumes along the line using the multigate approach previously described. Depending on the system employed, data from 250 to 500 points (or gates) along the beam line can be analyzed. Reflected ultrasound is simply analyzed at multiple times (corresponding to multiple gates) as a pulse train makes its way to, and back from, a given depth.

In the color flow processor, analysis of the filtered data from the quadrature detector is then finally performed. This analysis cannot be accomplished in the same way as is conventional pulsed Doppler, since multiple pulse trains are required for sampling in conventional pulsed Doppler. For example, up to 128 pulse trains may be required using the Fast Fourier Transform method employed by some pulsed systems. Since color flow systems must acquire data from thousands of gates throughout the entire field of view, they do not have the luxury of spending enough time in one place to deliver and receive such a high number of pulse trains. Thus, alternate means of analysis, based on fewer data, are required to construct a two-dimensional flow map.

These data are analyzed in color flow mapping by utilizing one of two mathematical approaches. The methods are known, respectively, as "autocorrelation" and "instantaneous frequency estimation" (Fig. 3–10). Some systems use a combination of the two methods which we have termed a "hybrid." These methods are very difficult to understand and have minimal impact on the conduct of an examination. Simply stated, all make a frequency shift estimate for each gate along a given beam line.

This frequency shift information from each sample gate obtained from successive pulse trains along the same beam line is also stored. The phase shift information is then assigned a velocity and color in the color flow processing section of the system for each packet (or series of pulse trains). Figure 3–11 simply demonstrates this process in a system using three phase shift estimates that result from a pulse packet size of 5. Mean velocity data returning from a given pulse train are simply called a sample. The mean of the frequency shift estimates obtained from the multiple pulse trains for each gate is then determined and displayed as one color in each gate at any point in time.

The Price of Compromise

As noted above, the more pulse trains in a given line (higher packet size), the better will be the mean estimate of flow for each gate. Too small a packet size will likely result in

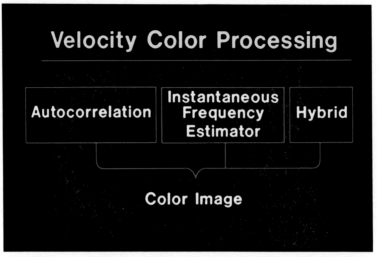

Fig. 3–10. There are a variety of complex methods for processing the Doppler data to develop the color image. For details, see text.

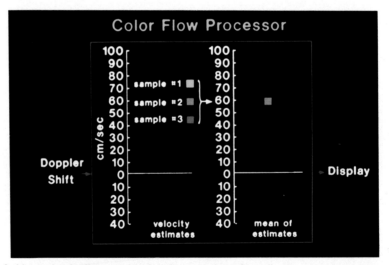

Fig. 3–11. A simple diagram showing the operation of a color flow processor where data from three pulse trains are used to estimate velocity and one mean estimate is finally displayed in the gate.

unreliable flow data. As explained previously, the minimal usable packet size is 3. Too large a packet size will result in too much time being devoted to each line, and frame rate or line density or sector angle will be sacrificed. Nominally, most systems have a packet size of be-

tween 6 and 8.

The time taken for various flow map systems to create this two-dimensional image of flow is variable. To move quickly, and thus maintain rapid frame rates, color flow operation requires fewer samples to be collected and processed

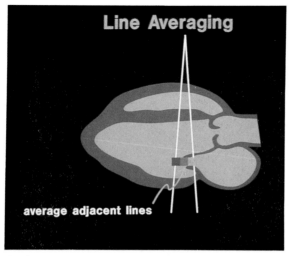

Fig. 3–12. At the far ranges gates are separated due to divergence of the radial scan lines. Data from adjacent gates are averaged to smooth the image.

and the resultant displayed velocity estimates are made less reliable. Echocardiographers have grown accustomed to conventional two-dimensional imaging where frame rates of 30 frames/sec preserve the smooth movement of the valves and walls. For color flow, taking more time enhances the reliability of the velocity estimates but compromises the frame rate. It may, in fact, drop as low as 4 or 6 frames/sec. This might create a situation that makes analysis of data quite difficult when flow is rapid, when rapidly moving anatomic targets are involved, or when heart rates are high as seen in neonates. Taking less time degrades the reliability of the flow velocity estimates but may be accomplished at much higher frame rates (more than 20 frames/sec). It is possible to have packet sizes as high as 16 but this size is impractical for cardiac imaging as the time taken to collect the data would be much too long and frame rates would be exceedingly low.

By sacrificing completeness of velocity information at each point, we are able to determine only mean velocity, but at many points. As the ultrasound line sweeps through the sector arc, mean velocity is determined throughout the field of view. All of this velocity information is then converted to color and finally combined with the anatomic image. This leads to the display of a cineangiogram-like picture of intracardiac blood flow.

Line Averaging

As the ultrasound lines diverge into the far field of the image they become more separate. At some point in space they are so separate that the resultant image would appear broken. To overcome this problem, data from a gate on one line are averaged with data on the adjacent line (Fig. 3–12). This process is repeated for each frame of color data throughout the field of view. The resultant averaging smoothes the appearance of colors in the final display and is also called "interline interpolation." This type of processing also is applied to the two-dimensional anatomic data as well.

Aliasing in Color Flow

As with conventional pulsed Doppler, aliasing occurs when using color flow methods. The reasons for this are identical to those previously described in Chapter 2. Like conventional

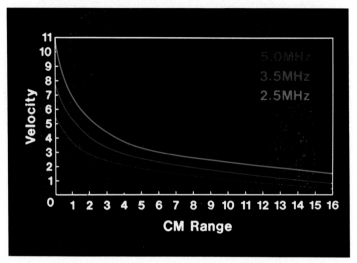

Fig. 3–13. The maximum velocity able to be recorded without aliasing at any range is a function of the frequency transmitted. For details, see text. (After material from Hewlett-Packard, Inc.)

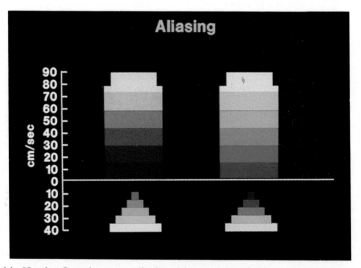

Fig. 3–14. If color flow data were displayed in a spectral format, aliased flow toward the transducer would not only be cut off at the top but the aliased flow into the opposite channel would be reversed in color. When flow toward the transducer is in red, aliasing would be into blue. The opposite would occur if flow toward the transducer was in blue.

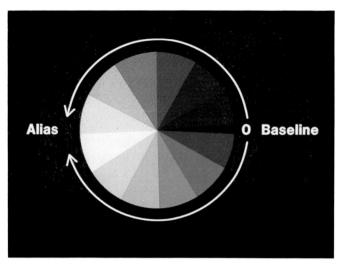

Fig. 3–15. Understanding of the importance of aliasing in the color flow image is best accomplished with a color wheel. Baseline, or zero, flow is displayed in black. High mean velocity data are aliased between brighter hues of red and blue and may be easily recognized in the final display.

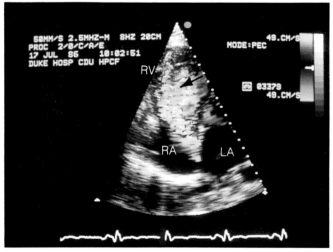

Fig. 3–16. Modified apical four-chamber view of flow through an atrial septal defect and into the tricuspid orifice in diastole. The bright yellow flow aliases into bright blue within the central core of the flow jet (arrow). This is an enhanced map.

pulsed Doppler, both depth and transducer ultrasonic frequency will determine the actual velocities at which aliasing occurs (Fig. 3–13). This graph demonstrates the peak velocity limit that can accurately be recorded at different depths for different frequency transducers. The farther into the tissue, the lower the velocity that can be accurately displayed. Lower-frequency transducers provide for more accurate recording of higher peak velocities at any given depth. Similar relationships exist when mean velocity estimates are measured. For color flow Doppler, these aliasing limits are set by maximum depth of field and not by the depth of any given gate. Less aliasing would be encountered when using lower-frequency transducers than with those of higher frequency.

The color correlates of aliasing are shown in Figure 3–14. In the red-toward mapping schema this would be displayed as a reversal of flow into the opposite direction and displayed as blue. In the blue-toward mapping scheme, the opposite would occur.

It is best to think of aliasing as a color wheel with zero flow at the right and represented as black. Figure 3–15 shows such a color wheel with zero flow on the right. An enhanced rendition of colors where the hues of red and blue are accentuated into very bright colors is used to aid the beginner in understanding the principle. For the differences between a standard red–blue map and the enhanced red–blue map refer back to Figure 1–4. In either direction, as the progressive mean velocities rise, brighter and brighter colors are progressively encountered until the aliasing point is reached at which there is a reversal of color into the opposite directional channel. Note that at the aliasing point the brightest hues of red and blue are adjacent. This fact aids the eye in the recognition of aliasing in the final display.

Aliasing is frequently associated with higher velocities and turbulent flow as are found in disease states. On the color display, as the signal is aliased from one color to the next, it appears as a mosaic of the very bright hues at the aliasing point. Figure 3-16 demonstrates the large mosaic encountered in a jet from an atrial septal defect as it moves through the right atrium and tricuspid valve into the right ventricle in diastole. The red flow toward the transducer aliases into bright shades of blue. An

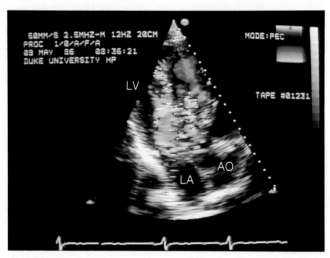

Fig. 3–17. Apical two-chamber view in diastole from a patient with severe aortic insufficiency. High-velocity regurgitant flow into the left ventricle is aliased between red and blue, making the abnormal jet readily recognizable.

apical two-chamber view of aortic insufficiency is seen in Figure 3–17 where the same phenomenon occurs. Note that the brightest of the colors red and blue are adjacent to one another indicating the aliasing point. The dullest of the colors are also adjacent to one another indicating the zero flow point.

While aliasing is a tremendous problem for conventional pulsed Doppler echocardiography it is less so for color flow. Because the aliasing is displayed in two dimensions as a mosaic, it frequently allows one to recognize areas of turbulence associated with disease states readily. Aliasing is, therefore, frequently used to advantage in the color flow map since it may dramatically highlight the presence of abnormal high velocities.

On the other hand, users of color flow need to become accustomed to aliasing within the image. Because analysis of large amounts of returning data from a two-dimensional scan is time consuming, the maximal PRF which can be utilized is relatively low. Because of this, aliasing may occur not only in the presence of pathologically high-velocity flow, but also in the presence of normal flow. As a consequence, some aliasing is present on most flow maps even if only normal velocities are present. This often distracting and may confuse interpretation.

The varying effect of transducer frequency on the aliasing phenomenon is demonstrated in the images of left ventricular outflow in a normal individual. Figure 3–18A shows the appearance of normal left ventricular outflow in a normal individual imaged at 2.5 MHz. At 3.5 MHz (Fig. 3–18B) the same velocities are assigned a brighter color in the display. At 5.0 MHz, the effect of aliasing is so profound as to actually reverse the color of almost the entirety of the outflow tract into blue (Fig. 3–18C).

The aliasing point for color flow systems is also dependent upon the maximum range of the field of view selected. As explained in Chapter 2, conventional pulsed Doppler systems will have variable aliasing points depending upon the location of the sample volume in the field. The farther the sample volume is located from

the transducer, the longer the time of flight of the pulse to and from the sample site in reference to the transducer. The longer the time (or the lower the PRF), the lower the velocity at which aliasing will occur. For color flow imaging, the same principle applies, but its effect in the final image is a bit different from that produced by conventional systems. In color systems the maximum pulse repetition frequency is set by the *maximum* overall depth selected. This influences *each* gate in the entire image field and is independent of whether the gate is near or far from the transducer. More aliasing will be seen throughout the image when scanning at deep scan range settings than at shallow scan range settings.

The implications for this in clinical scanning are significant. The highest-resolution ultrasound scanning is done with higher-frequency transducer systems. Yet, these frequencies have the greatest problem with aliasing. In small children, with rapid flow rates, aliasing may present tremendous interpretive difficulties differentiating normal (but aliased) flow and abnormal (but aliased) flow. These matters will be discussed later.

Variance

In some of these difficult states, detection and display of variance are helpful in differentiating the complex flows. In laminar flow, mean velocity is very close to peak velocity. As seen in Chapter 2, the velocity spectrum is narrow. In turbulent flow, the velocity spectrum is broadened with many different velocities being presented at any one time.

Color flow systems can, however, present only one color at any one gate. In an attempt to present turbulence in the color image, methods have been developed to detect this spectral broadening. This is usually referred to as "variance detection." Variance expresses the degree to which velocities within a given sample volume differ from the mean velocity within that sample (Fig. 3–19). The more the velocities differ within a sample volume, the greater will

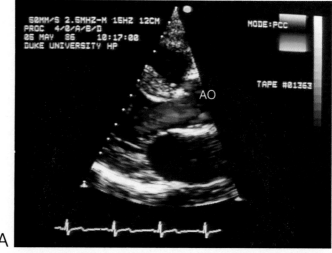

Fig. 3–18. The color appearance of flow is dependent upon the frequency of the transducer used. (**A**) A parasternal long-axis systolic image from a normal patient is seen using a 2.5-MHz transucer where outflow is imaged in dull hues of red. (*Figure continues.*)

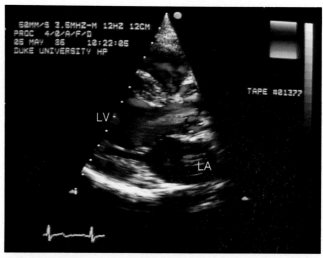

Fig. 3–18 (*Continued*). (**B**) When a 3.5-MHz transducer is used aortic outflow is slightly brighter, but still in red. (*Figure continues.*)

be the variance. In this example of laminar flow, there is very little variance, or difference, in velocity about the calculated mean. Since turbulent flow is characterized by flow at multiple different speeds in many different directions, the variance in a region of turbulent flow is high. There are electronic variance estimation circuits within the color flow imaging system that detect variance around the mean and when present beyond a given point incorporate it into the display.

A better understanding of how variance is

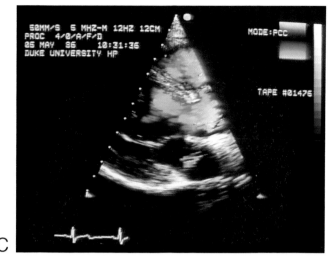

Fig. 3–18 (*Continued*). (**C**) When a 5.0-MHz transducer is used, all of the normal flow is aliased into bright blue.

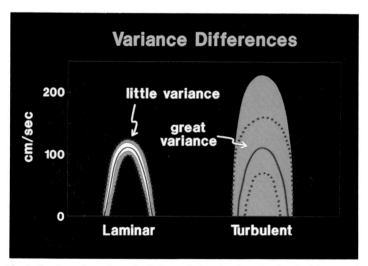

Fig. 3–19. In laminar flow there is little variation (variance) of velocities on either side of the mean velocity. In turbulent flow, when many different velocities are present, there is great variance.

displayed can be achieved by studying the color renditions in Figure 3–20A. In this figure, a standard color velocity display of direction (red or blue) and relative velocity (varying brightnesses of each color) for an aortic insufficiency jet are obtained from the apical approach. The accompanying color bars to the right of the image help to recognize which maps are being used.

Some systems have alternative maps where hues of the blues and reds are varied between brighter and less bright colors. In these, the

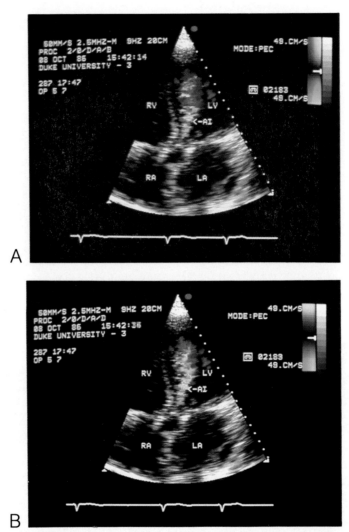

Fig. 3–20. Apical four-chamber diastolic view of aortic insufficiency demonstrating three different maps. The image is identical except for the map changes. (**A**) Red/blue map. (**B**) Enhanced map. (*Figure continues.*)

ranges of brightnesses are expanded to make the relative velocity data more different as seen in Figure 3–20B. This makes the higher peak velocities much more obvious in a vivid color image of abnormal flow. Most of these types of maps are without turbulence detection and may be generically referred to as color enhanced maps. Most of the previous figures and color illustrations are in the enhanced renditions to aid in recognition of velocity data. Again, the color bars to the right of the display help to

recognize this type of mapping scheme.

In most systems, shades of green are added when greater variance in blood velocity is present (when turbulence is greater). This results in the incorporation of green into the display as seen in Figure 3–20C. Here, the variance is seen overlaid on the map in Figure 3–20A.

The method chosen for the display involves the addition of the color green when variance is present (Fig. 3–21). Green is the third primary color of light. Since red and blue are al-

Fig. 3–20 (*Continued*). (**C**) Velocity/variance map. The flow image in Panel C superimposes the variance on top of the red/blue map in Panel A and identifies the regurgitant jet.

ready in the display, green is simply added "on top" of each of these colors. Forward flow with turbulance would result in yellow. Backward flow with turbulence results in a cyan (blue–green) color. Pure green is rarely present in the display. If multidirectional turbulence could be encountered at the same time, the result of all three colors would be white. If multidirectional flow without turbulence could be encountered, combinations of red and blue (without green) would result in magenta.

These intersecting color wheels have been presented to enhance the reader's understanding of the rules that govern the final color display. In reality, the red and blue circles do not intersect as color flow systems can assign only one color to a gate. Since the color is finally assigned to a mean velocity estimate it is either in the red or the blue direction. There is no true white or magenta in the final display.

It is important to recognize that a variance display in green can only be used with the standard red–blue map as baseline. Adding green to red and blue results in the various colors of yellow and cyan. Since these colors are already used in the enhanced map the addition of green would have no visible effect. Thus, yellow in an enhanced map only reflects velocity informa-

tion. Yellow in a variance map reflects turbulence.

Examples of the color bars reflecting different mapping schema are shown in Figure 3–22. Figure 3–22A shows four possible maps from the Aloka 880 system. At left is a simple red-toward/blue-away map without differences in brightness for velocity. It shows only direction and is rarely used. The next is a red-toward/blue-away map with progressive brightness added to indicate progressive increases in mean velocity. The third from the left is a velocity/variance map where green has been added to indicate turbulence. Here, hue and brightness are increased at the extremes of the color bar. The bar at the right does indicate velocity differences (variance off) but does not indicate direction and is rarely used.

Figure 3–22B shows possible maps from the Toshiba 65A system. The map at the left shows "power mode" and may be mistaken for direction and velocity while the map at the right is the velocity/variance map.

Maps from the Hewlett-Parkard system are in Figure 3–22C. The map at the left is the direction and relative velocity map. At the center is the enhanced map where the colors and hues are brightened to aid the observer's eye

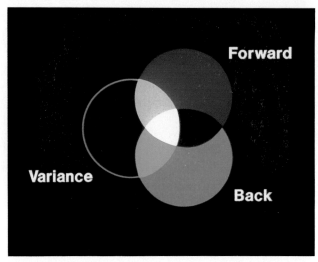

Fig. 3–21. When variance is detected, hues of green may be added to the red and blue flows resulting in shades of yellow, white, and blue–green (cyan).

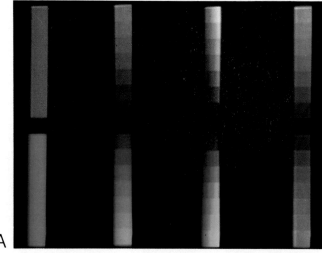

A

Fig. 3–22. Sample color bars of the various available maps from **(A)** the Aloka 880. (*Figure continues.*)

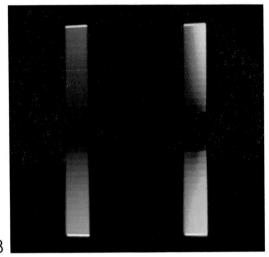

Fig. 3–22 (*Continued*). **(B)** The Toshiba 65A sample color bars. (*Figure continues.*)

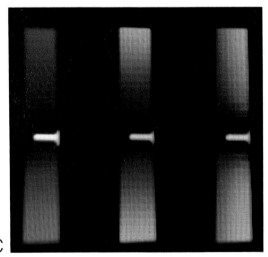

Fig. 3–22 (*Continued*). **(C)** Hewlett-Packard sample color bars. For details, see text.

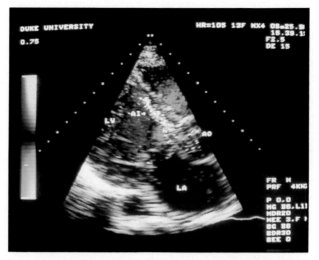

Fig. 3–23. Parasternal long-axis image in diastole showing the mosaic of highly turbulent aortic insufficiency where variance is present. Display of the bright colors and the addition of variance helps in the recognition of abnormal jets.

in detecting abnormal flow. At the right is a velocity/variance map.

When comparing system to system, the standard red–blue maps are roughly equivalent. On the other hand, the implementation of the amount of green added to the red–blue map when velocity/variance is displayed is totally arbitrary. No two systems have the same variance map. While variance contains important information for the user, the implementation into the final display can be thought of as cosmetic in nature. From this point on, we shall refer to the velocity/variance maps as variance only.

When turbulence is present, the range of mean velocities is broadened and variance is detected. The result in the display is a "mosaic" of reds, blues, yellows, and cyan in the turbulent area. Figure 3–23 shows the resultant mosaic of a very turbulent aortic insufficiency

jet. Turbulence is an important indicator of pathologic flow such as would be encountered in valvular regurgitation, stenosis, and many other abnormal conditions.

Mechanical and Phased Array Scanners

For some time, it was thought that mechanical scanning systems could not be used to perform color flow analyses due to marked frequency artifacts introduced by the moving scan heads. While this may be true, some systems are currently under development that minimize this problem and may result in acceptable color flow images from mechanical scanning systems. Currently, since phased array systems have no such problem they are the most common type of color flow systems in use.

4

The Role of the Various Doppler Methods

The Role of Conventional Pulsed Doppler

Conventional pulsed Doppler is able to precisely locate abnormal flows in space but suffers because true velocity recordings are not possible because of aliasing. Using spectral displays, the timing of onset of a jet may be accurately recorded but accurate recording of peak velocities is impossible in most abnormal jets since these velocities are invariably high and aliasing results.

As a result, pulsed Doppler is commonly used to detect the location of turbulent jets such as valvular insufficiency or shunts between the cardiac chambers. Most users of conventional pulsed Doppler would agree that the examination is laborious and excessively long, as it requires tedious mapping to identify the location and size of an abnormal jet.

Conventional pulsed Doppler does have a unique role for the location of abnormal flow or the timing of flow events. The spectral velocity tracing is mandatory for calculation of flow velocity integrals if cardiac output or other measurements are made.

The Role of Conventional Continuous-Wave Doppler

Conventional continuous-wave Doppler is able to record very high velocities but suffers because it is not possible to precisely locate the jet in space. As will be seen, this method is ideal for precisely quantitating transvalvular gradients or other quantitative manipulations based upon peak velocity determinations. It is the only Doppler method where such high peak velocities can be readily detected. Most users would indicate that technical mastery of the technique is difficult and time consuming.

The Role of Color Flow Imaging

Color flow imaging is based upon pulsed Doppler principles and, like conventional pulsed Doppler methods, cannot accurately record high-velocity information. Its unique advantage over conventional pulsed Doppler is that it displays the flow, normal and abnormal, directly onto the echocardiographic image. For those familiar with two-dimensional echo ap-

Fig. 4–1. The advantages of color flow imaging.

proaches, the pulsed Doppler examination may be quickly conducted using color flow. When compared with the conventional pulsed Doppler approach, the tedious mapping techniques necessary with the earlier techniques are avoided. Figure 4–1 summarizes the advantages of color flow imaging.

Because there is no spectral display, however, precise timing of events is not possible. Timing information is further complicated by the fact that it takes so long to create the two-dimensional color flow display. In addition, aliasing occurs at least as frequently as with conventional pulsed Doppler and peak velocities cannot be detected or identified in disease states. Figure 4–2 summarizes the disadvantages of color flow imaging.

The Combined Roles of Doppler Methods

Given all this information delineated in previous chapters, it appears that Doppler color imaging has an important role with the conventional approaches. In sensitivity (the ability to detect flow) it appears just as good as conventional pulsed methods. Conventional continu-ous-wave Doppler, because it is constantly interrogating and receiving, is, in most experienced operators' hands, the most sensitive.

Color flow methods are roughly quantitative of the size and direction of the abnormal jets. More precise quantitative work, such as derivations of measurements from peak velocity information, however, remain within the province of continuous-wave Doppler.

There is no question that the basics of color flow mapping may be learned reasonably quickly by experienced users of two-dimensional echocardiography. Pulsed Doppler requires a longer learning time. Continuous-wave Doppler requires the longest time in order to gain the experience to perform a proper examination.

The examination time required for a color flow examination is relatively short in comparison with the other methods. Simply switching color on and off as the two-dimensional examination is performed can reveal useful information in a very short period of time. A pulsed Doppler examination takes longer. Continuous-wave Doppler frequently is the most time consuming. A table summarizing the uses of the various Doppler methods is shown in Figure 4–3.

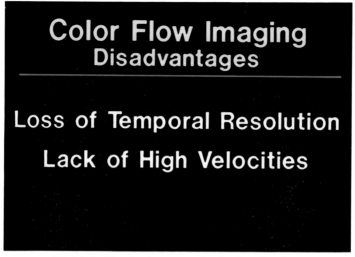

Color Flow Imaging
Disadvantages

Loss of Temporal Resolution

Lack of High Velocities

Fig. 4–2. The disadvantages of color flow imaging.

Doppler Roles

	CF	PW	CW
Sensitivity	good	good	best
Quantitative	semi	semi	best
Learning time	short	longer	longest
Examination time	short	longer	longest

Fig. 4–3. Table comparing color flow (CF), pulsed-wave (PW), and continuous-wave (CW) Doppler.

Integrating the Doppler Examinations

The most frequent indications for Doppler examinations in our laboratory are for the detection and rough quantification of valvular regurgitation and the detection of congenital cardiac defects. In almost all these cases, the color flow examination is quickly conducted simply by switching the color flow on and off as routine views are obtained. If normal, the examination is concluded without resorting to the other conventional methods. If abnormal, and/or if a question of precise timing of events is required, we proceed to the conventional pulsed Doppler approach. The color flow reveals the map of the area and direction of abnormal jets easily and does not require the time-consuming process of mapping needed with conventional pulsed Doppler.

By directly imaging a stenotic valve jet with color flow mapping, proper orientation of the continuous wave transducer may be facilitated. Orientation will be easier and is more likely to be accurate if an eccentric jet is encountered and identified on the color flow map. If the jet is abnormal, and a need arises for precisely recording an elevated peak velocity (such as when valvular stenosis is suspected), a continuous-wave examination is then conducted.

Thus, in routine clinical practice, color flow replaces conventional pulsed Doppler echocardiography in most, but not all, cases. Despite its increased cost, its ease of use, and relatively rapid technical mastery has resulted in considerable savings of time and patient cost. While it remains our feeling that a complete Doppler examination of the heart requires all Doppler methods, the advent of color flow has placed the conventional approaches into specific perspectives, now much more readily understood by even beginners in the use of Doppler techniques.

5

The Use of the Color Flow Controls

The Doppler Color Flow Examination

This discussion of the color flow examination assumes that the reader has covered the previous four chapters but requires no previous experience with Doppler methods. It does require that the user be readily familiar with the basics of two-dimensional echocardiography.

The color flow examination is most easily accomplished during the two-dimensional examination when there is a suspicion that any abnormal flow state exists, such as valvular regurgitation or communication between the cardiac chambers. The color flow may be readily switched on and off as the operator proceeds with the two dimensional examination as the various routine, or other pertinent views, are obtained. Conducting a separate color flow examination after the normal two-dimensional examination is, to us, unnecessarily time consuming.

As will be demonstrated in later chapters dealing with specific clinical problems, each cardiac valve can be quickly examined and various congenital abnormalities evaluated. Operators skilled in the two-dimensional echocardiographic examination should find it relatively easy to acquire the skills to perform color flow examinations.

A major point to keep in mind is that of proper transducer orientation. For conventional pulsed and continuous-wave Doppler, it is always best to be as parallel to flow as possible. This allows acquisition of the most accurate peak velocity information. Thus, accurate recording of mitral or tricuspid insufficiency is frequently best accomplished using the apical approach. These regurgitant jets are often directed parallel to the transducer beam in this view.

Although it may be said that the requirement for parallel orientation also applies to the color flow approach, the necessity is not as absolute. In fact, many valvular and other lesions may readily be detected from approaches not directly suited to the conventional approaches. Figure 5–1 demonstrates the appearance of mitral regurgitation as easily recognized from the left parasternal long-axis approach.

There are multiple reasons why direction of orientation is less important for the detection of abnormal flows using the color Doppler approach. First, in abnormal jets there are eddy currents moving in all directions. Even from the parasternal approach, aortic and mitral insufficiency may, therefore, be detected. Second, it is well known that a *complete* peak velocity profile of an abnormal jet cannot readily be detected on conventional spectral Doppler

51

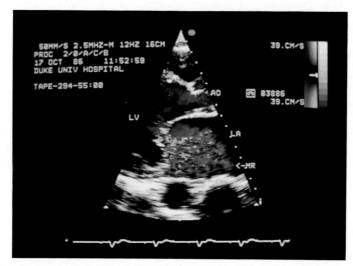

Fig. 5–1. Systolic parasternal long-axis color flow image of mitral regurgitation. Recognition of abnormal jets does not always require that the interrogating beam be parallel to the flow. A variance map is used. See text for details.

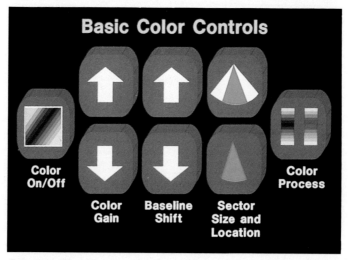

Fig. 5–2. Simplified Doppler color flow imaging controls. For details, see text.

displays unless the interrogating beam is nearly parallel to flow. When the conventional Doppler beam intercepts an abnormal jet in a nearly perpendicular angle some disturbed flow may be detected, but the velocity is very low and may render interpretation difficult. The same situation exists for color flow. Fortunately, color flow systems display information in space and in time, making recognition of the abnormal flow possible even when the mean velocity estimates are poor. It is the recognition of the presence of an abnormal jet rather than its absolute velocity content that brings color flow methods into clinical use.

In general, the operator eventually learns to use the two-dimensional display as a guide to detect the flow, and ultimately to make the final angulations necessary to optimize visualization of the flow. Angulation of the transducer to optimize the flow image will occasionally lead to rather unconventional simultaneous two-dimensional images. The goal of color flow mapping is not to optimize the two-dimensional image. Some diminished quality in this image should be expected if the best flow data are to be obtained.

The various color flow controls should then be adjusted to obtain the best demonstration of flow and image quality for the individual patient and disease state encountered. For experienced users of two-dimensional echocardiography just beginning in color flow, the process is a series of trial and error. For users unacquainted with two-dimensional echocardiography the results may be disastrous because there is simply too much to master at one time. We strongly recommend that such users master the two-dimensional approach before attempting color flow.

From color system to color system, the color flow controls may be very simple (and readily recognized) or excessively complex and intimidating (and sometimes buried in pages and pages of software). We suggest that beginning users master just a few controls and evaluate their effect on the resultant image before attempting to delve deeper into the literally scores of options available. Figure 5–2 demonstrates

a sample control panel that incorporates the major, and most commonly used, controls available. Where possible, we have tried to illustrate the use of the various controls on the same patient.

Color On

Ready access to the "color on" control is absolutely essential as the operator obtains the necessary two-dimensional view and then goes back and forth between the on and off position as required. Mastery of this control requires little skill. A beginner should first start with a subject with fairly good image quality and a known valvular or other disorder. Simply obtaining a view of the valve involved, then switching the color on and off should provide a good beginning. Figure 5–3 demonstrates the same parasternal long-axis image without (Fig. 5–3A) and then with the color flow superimposed (Fig. 5–3B).

Color Gain

The next most important control is the "color gain." Optimal adjustment of the gain setting is an important component of the color flow examination. Too high a gain will result in excessive noise in the image and detract from image quality and interpretability. Too low a gain setting will diminish sensitivity of the system in detecting small flow disturbances. It will further make large flow disturbances appear smaller. In most systems, excess gain is readily recognized by the appearance of background noise and distortion in the continuity of flow. This obscures the flow data as seen in Figure 5–4A. In this view the spatial limits of diastolic flow through the mitral valve orifice is difficult to recognize and the low-velocity flows in the left ventricular outflow tract shift from color to color. Proper control of gain is achieved by going up or down until background noise is just eliminated from the image (Fig. 5–4B). Note that with proper gain there is continuity

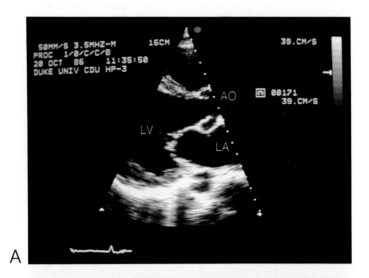

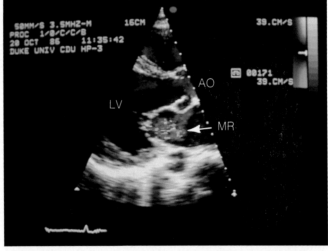

Fig. 5–3. (A) Parasternal long-axis view of two-dimensional echocardiogram. The color flow examination is readily conducted during the two-dimensional examination by switching the color on as each view is obtained. **(B)** Mitral regurgitation is seen with the color on. A variance map is used.

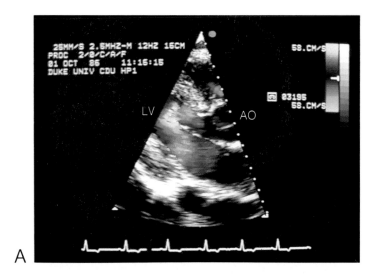

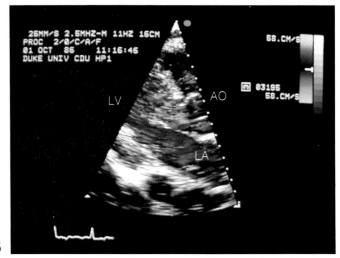

Fig. 5–4. Excessive use of color gain distorts the display of flow. **(A)** Normal mitral diastolic flow and filling of the left ventricular outflow tract distorted by excessive gain. **(B)** Proper use of gain where flows appear continuous. Enhanced maps are used.

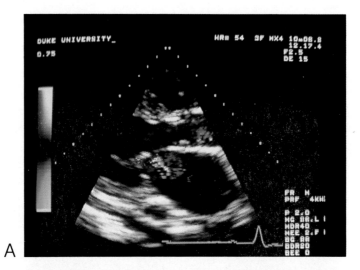

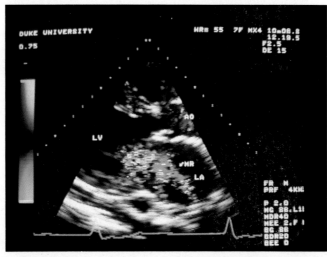

Fig. 5–5. Parasternal long-axis images of mitral insufficiency demonstrating the effect of color gain on the area of a regurgitant jet. **(A)** Too little color gain will underestimate the size. **(B)** Proper gain shows the regurgitant jet filling almost the entirety of the left atrium. Variance maps are used.

of flow in the display.

It is best for a beginner to work with a subject with a known, and readily identifiable, disorder. Progressively increasing and decreasing the gains should help one in obtaining skill with the gain control. Changes in color gain are not reflected on the color bar.

It must be recognized that the spatial representation of the limits of an abnormal flow jet is entirely dependent upon gain. Figure 5–5A

demonstrates a mitral regurgitant jet with too little gain. The area appears small. Slight increase in the gain reveals the full extent of the regurgitant jet (Fig. 5–5B) that fills virtually all of the left atrium. In our experience, it is quite difficult to make small jets abnormally large by the use of excess gain. It is, however, easy to make large jets appear very small by the lack of proper gain settings.

Most color systems will not map flow where

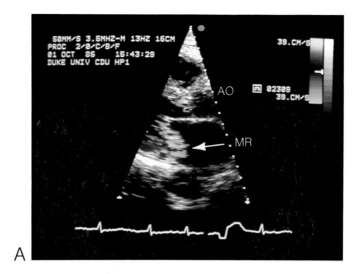

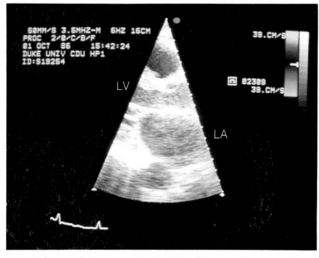

Fig. 5–6. Parasternal long-axis images of mitral insufficiency demonstrating the effect of image gain on the area of a regurgitant jet. **(A)** Proper image gain reveals the area of regurgitation directed toward the posterior wall of the left atrium. **(B)** Excessive image gain reduces the ability of the system to properly record the area of regurgitation.

there are target data on the display from the black and white image. It is *very important*, therefore, not to have excessive gain on the two-dimensional display before switching to color flow, as excessive gain on the anatomic image may obscure flow on the color display. In our experience, the most frequent error of operators of two-dimensional echocardiographic equipment is the excessive use of gain. This error will limit the appreciation of normal

or abnormal flows when switching into the color flow mode and is to be avoided.

Figure 5–6A shows a small mitral regurgitant jet directed toward the posterior wall of the left atrium. The two-dimensional gain settings are appropriate. The marked increase in two-dimensional gain in Figure 5–6B demonstrates how the use of excessive image gain obscures the color flow data and renders the mitral regurgitation almost unrecognizable.

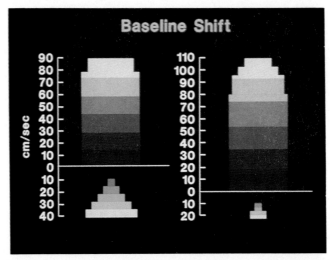

Fig. 5–7. Schematic diagram showing the effect of baseline shift in the color velocity display.

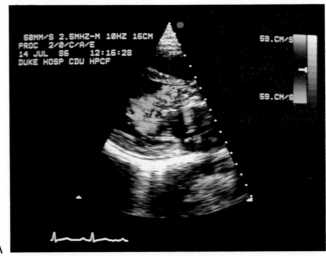

Fig. 5–8. Parasternal long-axis view of severe aortic regurgitation. (**A**) The baseline of the color flow bar in the center. (*Figure continues.*)

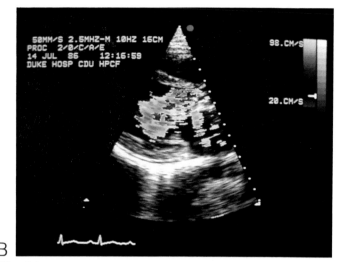

B

Fig. 5–8 (*Continued*). (**B**) The baseline lowered. (*Figure continues.*)

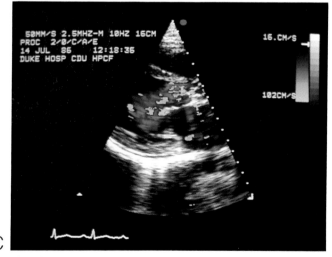

C

Fig. 5–8 (*Continued*). (**C**) The baseline raised. Baseline shift should rarely be used by beginners in color flow imaging. Enhanced maps are used. For details, see text.

Baseline Shift

A "baseline shift" control is found on most commercially available color flow systems. Sometimes prominently placed on the control panel, it moves the baseline colors up or down and keeps the colors as blue or red in an attempt to control aliasing. The effect of baseline shift on the colors is demonstrated in Figure 5–7 as the colors might be displayed on a conventional spectral Doppler recording. In an attempt to try to display only one color, the baseline is lowered and the colors that have wrapped into the opposite channel are progressively moved back into the forward, or red, color.

It is our recommendation that beginning users keep the baseline in the center until adequate experience has been obtained in the performance and interpretation of studies. The use of baseline shift before adequate experience only results in confusion for both the operator and interpreter due to the myriad of colors and presentations that result.

While we do not, at present, advocate the use of baseline shift for beginners, it does appear to help the final display of the various abnormal jets detected in the routine operating format. Figure 5–8 demonstrates a diastolic flow image of aortic insufficiency where the aliased signal of aortic insufficiency fills the aortic outflow tract (Fig. 5–8A). By shifting the baseline lower, all of the aortic insufficiency is presented in hues of red and yellow, making identification of the aortic insufficiency more obvious (Fig. 5–8B). Shifting the baseline upward leaves only hues of blue, rendering the aortic insufficiency less obvious (Fig. 5–8C).

Use of baseline shift frequently results in an effect that is opposite to what is first imagined. In these examples, aortic regurgitant flow is really away from the transducer and one would think that the flow would be most faithfully detected by taking maximum use of the entire range of mean velocities detected and displaying them in blue, since blue represents the velocity away from the transducer (Fig. 5–8C). While this may result in more recognition of the flow profile in a spectral display, in color

flow images this shifts the mean velocity data into less bright colors and renders the abnormal flow less recognizable. Shifting into the opposite channel (Fig. 5–8B) from flow brings the mean velocity data into the bright colors, making the disordered flow most recognizable. Thus, shifting the baseline opposite to what is obvious results in the most desired effect.

Sector Size and Location

Because there are marked compromises in frame rate when going into the color flow mode, most systems have automated controls that will decrease the size of the sector arc when color imaging is begun. Of the several choices available, the two most commonly used are the color image within a wedge of the full sector arc (Fig. 5–9A) and color within the entirety of a smaller sector arc (Fig. 5–9B) All choices are based upon the various compromises of frame rate discussed in Chapter 2.

As depth range and sector angle increase, more time must be devoted to sampling. As a consequence, other parameters must be sacrificed. Line density and/or frame rate must be diminished as sector angle and depth increase. Decreased line density will result in an image of diminished quality. Decreased frame rate will distort temporal changes in the Doppler flow pattern and make more difficult the interpretations of rapidly changing flows. Generally it is advisable to choose as small a depth range and sector angle as possible for the most faithful recording of flow data.

Increasing depth range will also decrease the pulse repetition frequency (PRF), which is determined by the total transit time from transducer to target and back. As PRF decreases, the Nyquist limit will also decrease. Thus, with a greater depth range aliasing will occur at lower velocities. Decreasing depth range will consequently decrease aliasing. This may be important since, as indicated previously, aliasing often occurs with normal velocities on the color flow map. If too pronounced, this phenomenon may obscure interpretation.

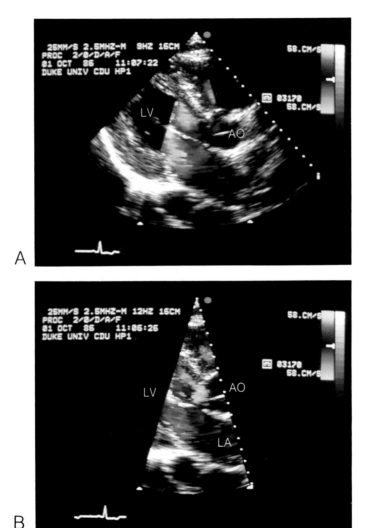

Fig. 5–9. Choices in sector size are available. **(A)** Parasternal long-axis image of normal mitral diastolic flow with a wedge of color in a large sector arc. Large displays reduce frame rate. **(B)** Same patient with a narrower sector arc. Enhanced maps are used.

Color Processing

Most systems allow a choice of the way in which color is used to display flow information. These color processing controls may be located on the same switch or key in some systems; in others, they may be located in several different locations on the control panel. As one might imagine from the previous discussions, many different process schema are utilized. To further confuse the situation, there is no standardization of the nomenclature for the various processing schemes available.

Color processing controls may be generically grouped into categories that provide choices of direction and turbulence/enhance displays, wall filters, spatial filters, color reject, and packet size. All have an effect in the final display.

In some systems the values are fixed and the choices are not as numerous. In systems where all are present they may be variably used together providing numerous and sometimes confusing choices. Some of these processing changes will result in a change in the appearance of the color bars that are displayed to one side or other of the final display.

We will detail the generic name of each group of process controls, explain their names, and show the effect on the color flow image. In each case we will recommend a starting process map to serve as a beginning place for those frightened by the many options. In addition, each manufacturer will supply recommended settings for getting started. Use of these many options is limited to special circumstances for enhancement of the flow image and it will take some time for the beginner to become accustomed to their use.

The simplified control panel shown in Figure 5–2 does not allow for all of these options since commercial systems have many varied implementations. Some require entry into special menus while others have more ready access by press buttons or switches. It is better for the reader to cover this chapter to become familiar with the effect of these controls. Once familiar, consultation with the manual provided with the user's system will help the user assess which controls are on the system and where they are located. Since names may change, it is most important to know the effect these controls have on the resultant image.

Direction and turbulence/enhance displays vary between systems. These may be generically referred to as the map controls. All have a method for displaying velocity data without turbulence detection. Flow direction is most frequently set with the red-toward/blue-away map. Since there is no absolute convention on this display, the alternate directional maps are included in some systems. Beginners should set the red-toward map and generally ignore the alternative. Changes in direction are always reflected on the color bars.

The details of use of these controls and their effect on the image were explained in Chapter 3. Beginners should locate and start with the turbulence map. When a patient with disordered flow is encountered it frequently helps a beginner to understand how the variance detection works by switching between the simple red/blue map and the variance map.

Wall filter processing controls may be changed in some systems. Baseline filter controls variably eliminate low-velocity flow information that results from the movement of the heart walls and valves. Without the use of these controls considerable artifact results in the image from the moving anatomic structures; this is referred to as ''ghosting'' and appears in the display as dull hues of red or blue depending upon the direction of movement of the given structure. Figure 5–10 demonstrates ghosting into hues of red of the lateral walls of the right ventricle, tricuspid ring, and right atrium as the heart descends toward the apex in systole. Changes in wall filter are generally not reflected on the color bars.

Early color flow system displays had considerable problems with ghosting. These maps may be referred to as ''additive'' as they add low-velocity data from the moving anatomic targets to the final display. These maps can cause considerable distraction to rapidly moving anatomic targets such as heart valves, vegetative masses, or intracardiac masses. Depending upon the size

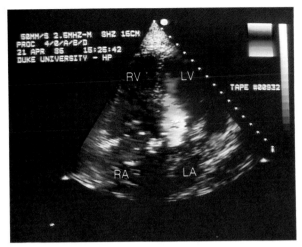

Fig. 5–10. Apical four-chamber view in systole where the portions of the right ventricular wall and tricuspid ring are assigned a color. This "ghosting" results when rapidly moving anatomic structures are encoded in color. Special wall filters in color systems reduce this problem.

of an orifice, use of an additive map may make location difficult, as colors are assigned to surrounding tissues.

Most newer systems have preset wall filter controls that reduce the ghosting artifact considerably. We have arbitrarily called some of these maps "exclusionary," as they exclude data from the moving anatomic structures. Exclusionary maps are really not based on true wall filter methods. Rather, they weight the relative strengths of the anatomic and flow signals, then display only the strongest so that there is no overlay of color on targets.

Figure 5–11 demonstrates an additive map of mitral regurgitation where color is taken up by both the regurgitant jet and the closed mitral valve leaflets (Fig. 5–11A). Figure 5–11B is of the exact same frame, but with an exclusionary map revealing the mitral valve orifice more readily (arrow). For most situations, exclusionary maps are generally preferred. Changes in wall filtering are not reflected on the color bars.

Spatial filtering is very complex and most systems have some spatial filter built in and preset. When available, filters act to smooth the color flow data, essentially averaging the data from adjacent flow gates in depth and laterally (or sometimes only in one of the two dimensions). The use of spatial filters also has the effect of reducing the very bright colors and elevating the very dull colors to a more uniform level of brightness.

Figure 5–12 demonstrates the effect of spatial filtering in the final display. Figure 5–12A shows a mitral regurgitant jet with the spatial filters off. Note the fine appearance of the mosaic in comparison to Figure 5–12B where the spatial filters are on.

When the spatial filters are off, system noise is more apparent and may be minimized by a slight reduction in overall color gain. To many users, the operation of the color system with the spatial filters off is preferential. The lack of spatial filtration makes the abnormal flow more readily apparent to the eye by retaining more discrete points in the mosaic and preserving the brightness of the aliased jet. Since there is so much degradation of quality in video recording, this effect is very much more noticeable in the videotaped image than in the original live display.

We recommend against the use of excessive

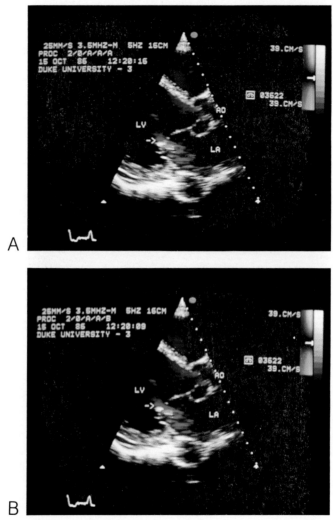

Fig. 5–11. Different processing controls are available in some systems to further separate flow from target data. **(A)** Mitral regurgitant jet where some color is assigned to the mitral valve leaflets obscuring the orifice of the regurgitant jet (arrow). **(B)** Alternate processing control where the subtle colors resulting from the valve leaflets are eliminated and the orifice is more obvious (arrow). Variance maps are used.

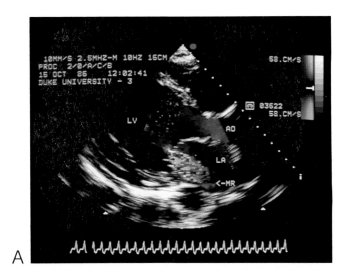

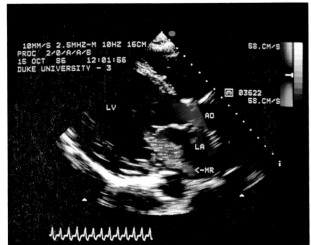

Fig. 5–12. Parasternal long-axis views of a mitral regurgitant jet showing the effect of spatial processing. **(A)** Without spatial processing; **(B)** with spatial processing. Spatial processing smooths the flow image at the expense of brightness in the turbulent mosaic. Variance maps are used.

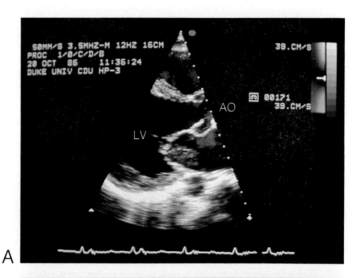

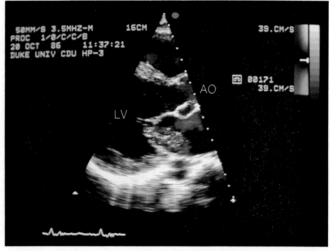

Fig. 5–13. Parasternal long-axis views of a mitral regurgitant jet showing the effect of color reject. **(A)** With high color reject; **(B)** with low color reject. High reject reduces system sensitivity but helps to eliminate noise in the display. Spatial filtering is used with variance maps.

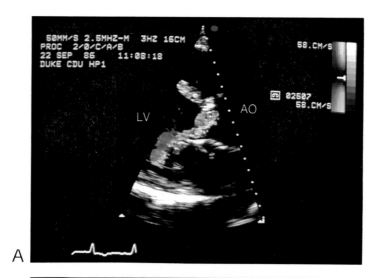

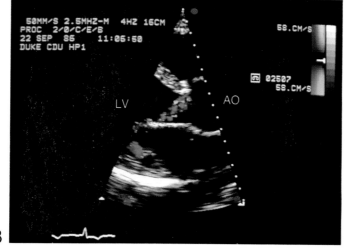

Fig. 5–14. Parasternal long-axis views of an aortic regurgitant jet showing the effect of packet size changes. **(A)** Acquired with large packet size and **(B)** with medium packet size. (*Figure continues.*)

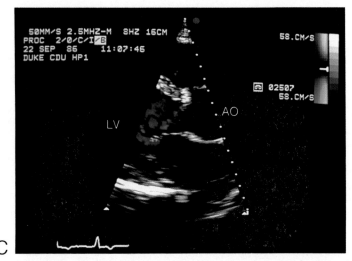

Fig. 5–14 (*Continued*). **(C)** Acquired with small packet size. Large packet sizes have the best estimates of mean flow but come at the expense of frame rate. Spatial filtering is used with variance maps.

spatial filtration for video recording for beginning users. Spatial filtration has no effect on the color bar.

Color reject is also available on some systems. When available it is a true reject that may be compared to the reject control found on old M-mode systems. Higher levels of reject will eliminate more and more low-level signals. Flow is better with a low reject level because more information is available. Figure 5–13A shows a mitral regurgitant jet with high reject. Low-velocity flows are not displayed as well as in Figure 5–13B, where low color reject is used. The price of low reject is more background noise in the image. With spatial filters on, the differences may be less noticeable. Most beginners should start at a low reject level. Changes in color reject are not reflected in the color bar.

Pulse sequence may also be changed in some systems. These controls change packet sizes, varying the number of pulse trains. Because more pulse trains per imaging line allow more sampling of each point along the line, more accurate estimates of flow velocity at each point can be made. This results in a better quality flow velocity image at the price of either lower frame rate or lower line density. The optimal setting will be one which allows easiest interpretation of the image by the individual sonographer. It is best to start with an individual manufacturer's recommended settings. Changes in pulse sequence are not reflected on the color bar.

The effects of higher and lower pulse packet sizes are seen in Figure 5–14. Figure 5–14A shows better detection of aortic regurgitant flow using the larger pulse packet size than when medium (Fig. 5–14B) or small (Fig. 5–14C) packet sizes are used.

Another subtle effect of differing packet sizes is seen in Figure 5–15, where mitral regurgitation is seen from the left parasternal long-axis view. Figure 5–15A was acquired with a large packet size and aliasing is readily appreciated in the center of the regurgitant jet. Figure 5–15B was acquired in the same individual with a medium packet size where less aliasing and less bright colors are seen. This results because smaller packet sizes provide fewer estimates for the calculation of mean velocity. The larger the packet sizes the better the final mean velocity estimate and recognition of an abnormal jet in the final display.

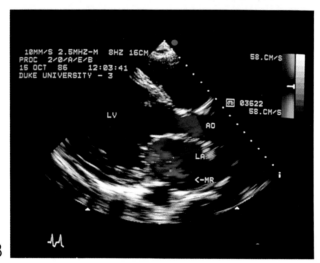

Fig. 5–15. Parasternal long-axis views of a mitral regurgitant jet showing the effect of packet size changes on the mean velocity estimates. **(A)** Acquired with large packet size, and bright colors and aliasing are seen within the abnormal jet; **(B)** acquired with medium packet size, and less bright colors are detected because of poorer mean velocity estimates. Spatial filtering is used with variance maps.

In our experience, control over packet size is very important. There are clinical situations in which higher frame rates (such as in infants) are required and smaller packet sizes are necessary to detect the abnormal flow, even though some sacrifice is made in the final display.

These many process choices may result in great confusion to the user and their improper use may seriously jeopardize the resulting image. In choosing the appropriate setting, the sometimes conflicting issues of visual quality and sensitivity must be balanced with each other. Most manufacturer's guides to any instrument use will recommend certain baseline setting as a starting point. Table 5–1 summarizes the effect of the various controls on the color

Table 5–1. Summary of System Controls

Control	Available on All Systems[a]	Effect Color Bar	Effect Frame Rate	Effect Flow SENS[b]	Comments
Color on/off	+	+	0	0	Color on for flow image
Color gain	+	0	0	+	Excess obscures flow
Color direction	0	+	0	0	Red-towards best for standard
Baseline shift	+	+	0	0	Keep at midlevel in beginning
Sector size	+	0	+	+	Large size sacrifices frame rate, small enhances SENS; keep at midlevel to start
Turbulence maps	+	+	0	0	Turbulence on is best starting place
Enhance maps	0	+	0	0	Use variably with turbulence
Wall filters	0	0	0	+	High filter sacrifices SENS but eliminates wall colors; start with some filter on
Spatial filters	0	0	0	+	High filter sacrifices SENS but smooths flow appearance; keep at low level to start
Color reject	0	0	0	+	High reject sacrifices SENS but decreases background noise; start with reject at midlevel
Packet size	0	0	0	+	Large size enhances SENS but sacrifices frame rate; start at high level or midlevel.

[a] Available for operator control (in some systems these are not available at all or are preset)

[b] SENS = sensitivity

image and suggests a setting for beginners.

Once initial experience is gathered, we recommend that the user investigate each choice with an easily imaged subject to see the effect on the resultant image. Sometimes only the most experienced user can render the proper decision to maximize the final display. For beginners, returning to the recommended baseline settings is usually the best way to initiate a study.

Recording the Image

The final record of the color flow study is generally recorded on videotape for later playback and analysis. There is a serious degradation in image quality in the video recording process and the original image at the time of patient study is always better than the recorded playback. Videotaped images have a significant impairment in resolution and color brightness when compared with the original display. Perhaps the rapidly advancing field of video technology will overcome this problem in time.

Rapidly changing colors on the real-time display sometimes complicate interpretation. For this reason, playback on a video recorder equipped with slow-motion, still-frame, frame-by-frame forward and back capability is recommended. Some color systems have a cine-loop provision where one heartbeat may be recorded and played back at any speed or direction to assist the reviewer in interpreting the data.

Hard-copy devices such as instant films and printers also fail to render an acceptable facsimile of the original display. The quality of information conveyed in any still-frame image is, of course, highly dependent on the details of information captured for presentation. Such devices are added to systems for convenience's sake and rapid improvement in these devices may someday render them more practical.

Images presented in this text were captured

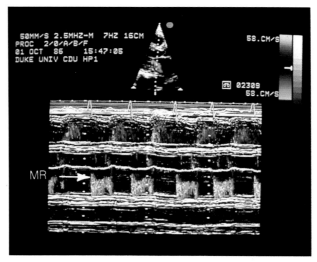

Fig. 5–16. Color M-mode of mitral regurgitation. Many optional displays are included in color flow devices and the most common is an M-mode display.

with the imaging system in freeze frame and then presented on a separate RGB (red-green-blue) color monitor. The use of a RGB monitor reduces the variations in color hue. The monitor was always set on "underscan" to reduce the effect of image distortion at the edges due to curvature of the monitor screen. The images were then recorded on color slide film by means of a 35-mm camera focused on the television monitor and set at an exposure time of $\frac{1}{4}$ second. Five exposures (from F 2.5 through F 11) were made and the best exposure selected. Unfortunately, this approach enhances the contrast of the blacks and whites of the two-dimensional anatomic data. Almost all images in this volume have excessive contrast of anatomic data in order to properly record the color data on film. This laborious process, in our opinion, is the best available method for recording hard copy until the advent of more convenient methods.

Other Combinations

Most color flow systems also have a color flow M-mode presentation. This allows for the freezing of the two-dimensional image and the presentation of line selectable M-mode with the color superimposed (Fig. 5–16). M-mode is sometimes very helpful for displaying information where critical timing of flow events is desired. Other combinations of controls such as use of combined color flow and conventional pulsed or continuous-wave Doppler will be discussed in later chapters as various disorders are presented.

6

Flow Patterns in the Normal Heart

The normal color flow examination of the heart produces many changing colors as the blood flows from chamber to chamber through the cardiac valves. Most normal velocities are relatively low (up to 1.5 m/sec) and when imaged in the adult at 2.5 MHz there is only occasional aliasing. This chapter is meant to familiarize the reader with some of the normal patterns of blood flow in the heart. We will begin with flow through the left heart since most readers are acquainted with the common views needed to interrogate these chambers.

For beginners with untrained eyes, normal events in the heart happen rapidly enough that at first try flow may simply appear as confusing flashes of color. It is sometimes helpful to videotape a short sequence and then go over it frame by frame to develop a better understanding of the rapidly changing events. Others may find the freeze-frame capability of any system useful. To accomplish this, the user would simply attempt to capture certain systolic or diastolic events and place the colors in the image together with the timing of known cardiac events.

In this chapter we demonstrate only some of the more important examples of normal forward flow through the heart. We also include a very detailed explanation of how flow is variably displayed in the color image.

Left Atrial Flows

During most of systole, the left atrium is usually without color. Figure 6–1 demonstrates this normal appearance and shows that during this portion of the cardiac cycle most of the left heart flow is from the left ventricle to the aorta.

One of the most surprising things about color flow Doppler is that pulmonary venous flow is readily obtained in many patients. Indeed, in our experience we had little idea of where the pulmonary veins were located in most adult patients until we began using color flow methods.

In the parasternal long-axis the low-velocity pulmonary venous flow is frequently seen emerging from the mid to upper portion of the left atrial wall. Figure 6–2 demonstrates the dull hues of red as this low-velocity pulmonary venous flow moves into the left atrium. This flow is frequently seen in systole as the atrium fills. Even more frequently, it is seen in early diastole as the blood is emerging from the pulmonary veins. Since the flow through the mitral valve is not yet maximum, the remainder of the left atrium has relatively little color.

As diastole progresses the atrium serves as a conduit for flow into the left ventricle. At this time, velocities are low and directions are varied. It is unusual to see the entirety of the left

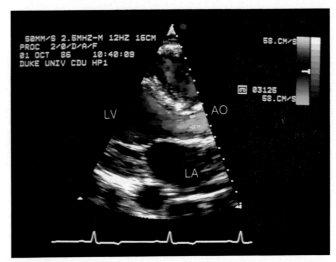

Fig. 6–1. Left parasternal long-axis showing normal aortic outflow and normal mitral valve coaptation. No mitral regurgitation is seen. The left atrium is relatively color-free. An enhanced map is used.

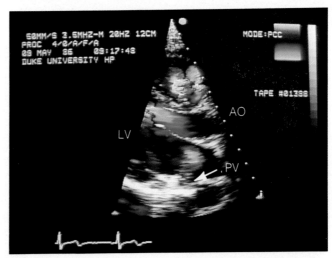

Fig. 6–2. Early diastolic image of pulmonary venous inflow as represented in red (arrow). Rarely is the left atrium filled during diastole. An enhanced map is used.

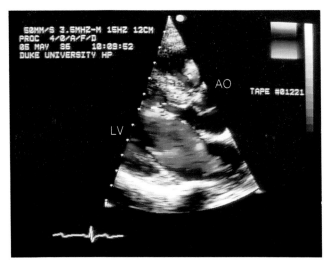

Fig. 6–3. Left parasternal long-axis of blood emerging from a pulmonary vein and filling the mitral valve orifice. An enchanced map is used.

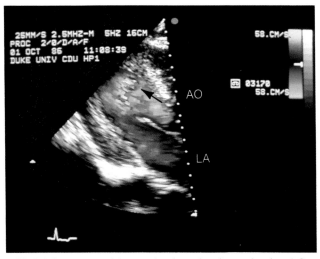

Fig. 6–4. Modified left parasternal long-axis view showing red colored flow toward the transducer and filling the left ventricle. As the blood curls around the mitral valve leaflet it shifts color into hues of blue (arrow). The image is in an enhanced map.

atrium filled with color at any time during diastole. Figure 6–3 shows low-velocity flow moving from a superior pulmonary vein through the mitral valve from the atrium during passive ventricular filling (during the first peak of the M-mode echocardiogram of the mitral valve). Similar events can be seen from different transducer positions such as the apical two- or four-chamber views.

Left Ventricular Inflow

As blood moves into the left ventricle and flow velocity is maximum in early diastole, aliasing rarely occurs when using a 2.5-MHz transducer. Most commonly the colors are not very bright, reflecting this low-velocity situation. Figure 6–4 shows the typical appearance of early diastolic flow into the left ventricle. A bit of aliasing is seen within the forward flow just adjacent to the septum. As the blood curls around the tip of the mitral valve and moves into the left ventricular outflow tract, the color shifts from red to blue as the result of a directional shift. Thus, the transition of

the colors is between dull hues rather than bright as is the case with aliasing.

From the apical approaches this transition in direction can also be seen as flow into the left ventricle shifts from red to blue as the flow curls around the apex. This phenomenon is readily seen in Figure 6–5. It is remarkable that flow can sometimes be followed in this portion of the cardiac cycle all the way from the pulmonary veins, through the mitral orifice, around the apex of the left ventricle and into the left ventricular outflow tract.

Left Ventricular Outflow

As ventricular systole begins, the aortic valve begins to open. Aortic valve opening is a very rapid event and is rarely imaged between the fully closed and fully open positions. Figure 6–6 is a rare image of flow as the aortic valve is only partially open and was obtained from an early prototype scanning device with a blue-toward map.

Flow through the aortic valve in systole is normally laminar. Since relatively low pulse

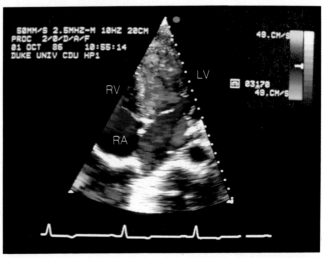

Fig. 6–5. Apical four-chamber view of normal pulmonary venous inflow through the mitral valve and curling around the apex of the left ventricle. Again, the color shifts from red to blue as the directions of left ventricular filling are altered. The image was obtained using an enhanced map.

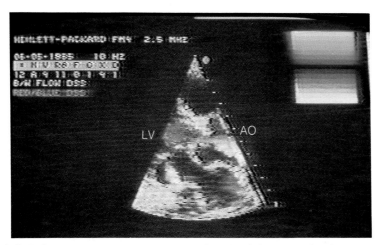

Fig. 6–6. Left parasternal long-axis view showing blood flow emerging from a partially open aortic valve. It is exceedingly rare to capture such an image. A blue-toward enhanced map was utilized in this prototype system.

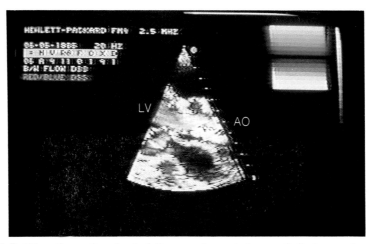

Fig. 6–7. When the aortic valve is fully opened a central core of aliasing can be seen at peak systole in some patients. This image was obtained from a prototype system using a blue-toward enhanced map.

repetition frequences are utilized in color flow mapping, velocities in the left ventricular outflow tract during systole frequently lead to Doppler shifts which exceed the Nyquist limit and aliasing results. In addition, velocities in the center of the aorta are slightly higher than in adjacent areas since friction forces tend to decrease velocity of blood adjacent to the vessel wall. As a result, a central core of aliased flow may be occasionally seen within the aorta as mean velocities exceed the Nyquist limit during peak systole. Figure 6–7 demonstrates such a central core of aliasing from the same prototype system just mentioned.

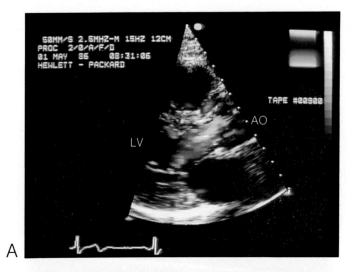

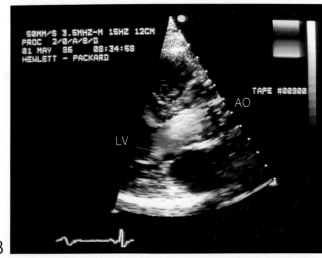

Fig. 6–8. (**A**) Left parasternal long-axis of left ventricular outflow using a 2.5-MHz trans-ducer. A tiny central core of aliasing is seen. (**B**) Same patient, viewed using a 3.5-MHz transducer. The aliasing is now more marked. The appearance of any blood flow will alter depending on transducer frequency. Enhanced maps were used.

Transducer frequency can markedly alter the color flow image of flow as was described in detail in Chapter 3. Figure 6–8 shows normal aortic outflow with a 2.5-MHz-frequency trans-ducer where a slightly higher mean velocity is seen in the center of the laminar flow as a brighter hue of red (Fig. 6–8A). Figure 6–8B demonstrates the appearance of aortic outflow in the same patient using a 3.5-MHz transducer where a central core of aliasing is seen. Lower-frequency transducers always give less aliasing.

When the left ventricular outflow tract is im-aged from the apex, aliasing of flow is almost always seen during systole with any standard frequency transducer. Imaging the outflow tract from this position usually requires an increase in the depth scale and consequently results in a further drop in pulse repetition frequency.

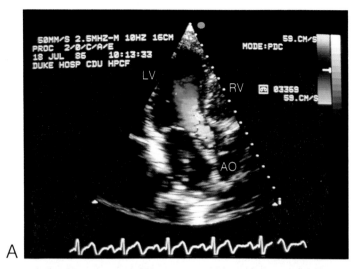

A

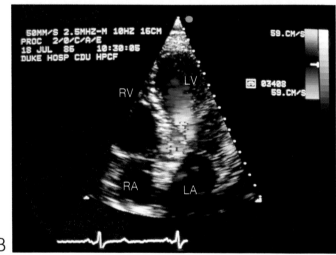

B

Fig. 6–9. (A) Apical two-chamber view of normal left ventricular outflow. Diffuse aliasing is always seen when examining this area at distant ranges. **(B)** Similar phenomenon in an apical four-chamber view. Both images were obtained using 2.5-MHz transducers. Enhanced maps were used. For details see text.

Such examples of normal aliasing are seen in Figure 6–9 where the outflow tract flow is seen from the apical two- (Fig. 6–9A) and four- (Fig. 6–9B) chamber views. Despite all of this aliasing, turbulence in the normal heart is rarely seen when variance maps are used.

In the short-axis view of the aorta, normal flow can be seen filling the aortic valve orifice in some patients. Figure 6–10 demonstrates the appearance of normal aortic outflow in a variance map. Little aliasing is seen in this view since the maximum scan depth is rather shallow. In addition, the dull hues of red indicate that relatively low mean velocities were calculated in this situation due to the rather perpendicular orientation of the interrogating beam with the aorta.

Occasionally, flow may be seen in the coro-

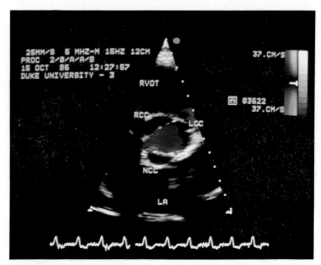

Fig. 6–10. Parasternal short-axis view of flow through a fully open aortic valve as it fills the aortic orifice. A variance map was used.

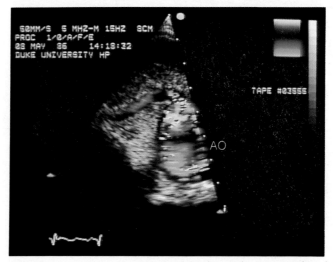

Fig. 6–11. Parasternal short-axis view of blood in the aortic root entering the proximal right coronary artery. The aortic root is severely aliased due to use of a 5-MHz transducer. As the blood enters the coronary artery and becomes perpendicular to flow no signal is obtained. As it moves away color is shifted from red to blue. An enhanced map was used.

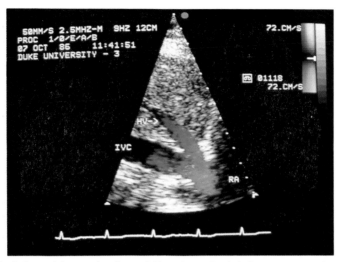

Fig. 6–12. Subcostal long-axis view of flow from the inferior vena cava into the right atrium. A variance map was used.

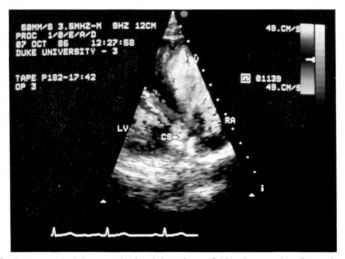

Fig. 6–13. Parasternal right ventricular inlet view of blood emerging from the coronary sinus and filling the right atrium. An enhanced map was used.

nary arteries. Figure 6–11 shows a color flow image of a normal proximal right coronary artery. The flow in the aorta is severely aliased due to the use of a 5-MHz transducer. As the flow enters the coronary artery it appears red. As it proceeds perpendicular and then away, the color is shifted through the baseline to blue.

Right Atrial Inflow

Analogous events may be observed in the right-sided chambers, though flows are of lower velocity, and less intense coloration (brightness) will be seen. With the transducer in the subcostal position, flow may be seen to enter the right atrium from the inferior vena cava and hepatic veins. Figure 6–12 shows the diastolic flow in blue. Similar detection of flow may be made from the superior vena cava with proper transducer orientation. Figure 6–13 shows coronary sinus flow entering the right atrium in the right ventricular inlet view and sometimes helps to locate the position of this anatomic structure in the image.

Right Ventricular Inflow

Right ventricular inflow may be imaged in any appropriate view including the apical four-chamber view, the left parasternal short-axis, or the right ventricular inlet view. Figure 6–14 shows the typical low-velocity appearance of blood flow emerging from the inferior vena cava and moving into the right ventricle through the open tricuspid valve. Note that flow in the right ventricle curling toward the outflow tract at the upper right exhibits a color change corresponding to the direction.

Normal right-sided flow into the right ventricle rarely aliases when images are obtained using a 2.5-MHz transducer. When higher-frequency transducers are used, aliasing can be expected. Note the aliased flow just as blood is entering the right atrium from the inferior vena cava in Figure 6–15 when a 5-MHz transducer was used in a small child.

Right Ventricular Outflow

As blood emerges from the right ventricular outflow tract into the proximal pulmonary artery in systole, velocities are increased and aliasing frequently occurs. Figure 6–16A shows very early systolic flow into the main pulmonary artery. Figure 6–16B demonstrates the marked aliasing that occurs just an instant later in systole that is typical of normal right ventricular outflow. Note also that the flow can typically be detected to the bifurcation of the main pulmonary artery and occasionally into the right and left pulmonary arteries.

The Aortic Arch: Angle Dependent Flow Imaging

Doppler methods are totally dependent upon the relationship of the interrogating beam and the direction of blood flow. As was seen in previous chapters, the best recording of velocity is obtained when the Doppler beam is parallel to flow. If not parallel, lower velocities than exist will be spuriously measured. When this occurs with color imaging systems, the colors will change remarkably, dependent upon the angle between the beam and flow. This results in what may be termed "angle-dependent" images.

All other imaging methods of flow through the heart are free of angle dependency. The apical four-chamber views in Figure 6–17 demonstrate the visualization of blood flow in a conventional two-dimensional image using a 5-MHz transducer in a patient with a porcine mitral valve and low cardiac output. Such direct visualization of flow is not dependent upon the angle between the interrogating beam and the flow of blood as is the case with Doppler methods.

Such angle dependency represents a major limitation to the use and implementation of Doppler color flow imaging. Understanding of the phenomena involved is required for proper studies to be recorded and interpreted. This section contains important information necessary

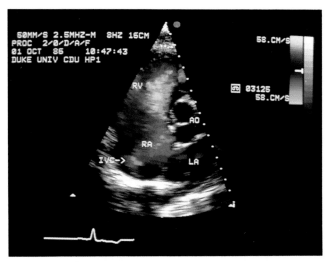

Fig. 6–14. Left parasternal short-axis view of the aortic root and right atrium. Low-velocity flow can be seen to emerge from the inferior vena cava and move through the right atrium and tricuspid valve into the right ventricle. Note that as the flow begins to fill the right ventricular outflow tract at the upper right, the color shifts from red to blue because of a shift in direction. An enhanced map was used.

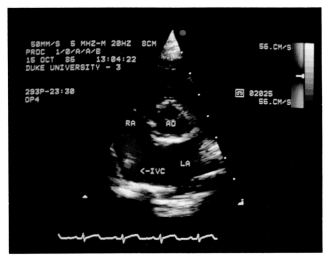

Fig. 6–15. Parasternal short-axis view of aliased flow entering the right atrium from the inferior vena cava using a 5-MHz transducer. When high-frequency transducers are used aliasing will occur even for very low-velocity flows. A variance map was used.

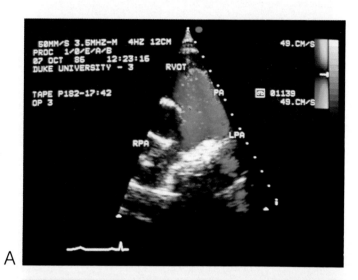

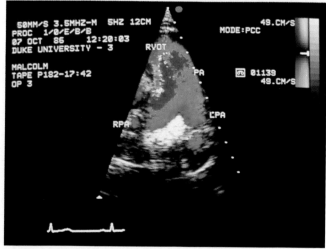

Fig. 6–16. Parasternal short-axis views of the aortic root showing the pulmonary outflow tract. **(A)** Flow in very early systole as it fills the proximal pulmonary artery to the bifurcation. **(B)** Flow an instant later when marked aliasing normally occurs. Variance maps were used.

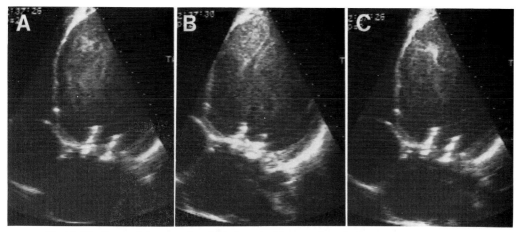

Fig. 6–17. Sequential conventional black and white two-dimensional images from the apex of the left ventricle in a patient with low cardiac output and a procine mitral valve. Using a 5-MHz transducer the flow can occasionally be seen in some patients. This flow is not angle-dependent. For details see text.

to understand images that are angle dependent. A reader should return to this section several times to acquire a thorough appreciation of angle dependency. In our experience, very few individuals truly understand this concept.

A normal color flow image of the ascending aorta is the best view where angle dependency is demonstrated, although angle dependency exists in every color flow image. Flow imaging in the aortic root can be accomplished as frequently as the ascending aorta and aortic arch can be visualized in normal adults. Figure 6–18 shows a systolic flow image of the aortic arch from the suprasternal approach. It is striking that the colors and hues are so varied when it is recognized that flow is laminar and of a uniform velocity throughout the arch. Careful study of this particular image will help the beginner understand the vagaries of the color flow display.

The color data in this image were collected in just a fraction of a second and do not represent sequential flow around the arch. Flow in the ascending aorta is in red, then shifts to blue across the arch as the direction of flow changes

relative to the transducer. Between these color shifts is an area displayed in black. For each color, the hues vary between dull and bright. Just after the arch there is an area of color shift from bright blue to bright yellow. A detailed explanation of these multiple colors will demonstrate how the basic physical principles of system operation determine the varied appearances of normal and abnormal flow.

Explanation of this flow image begins with the recognition that the transducer is stationary on the chest wall and it is the blood that is moving. Flow approaching from the ascending aorta on the left is relatively parallel to the Doppler beam and is represented in brighter hues of red. In this situation, the angle between the beam and the flow is 0 and the cosine is 1. Because the beam is parallel to the flow, estimates of mean flow are more reliable.

The red flow approaching the area where the beam is perpendicular shifts into progressively duller hues as the angle between the beam and the flow is increased. When the beam is finally perpendicular (90 degrees) to the flow, the cosine of the angle is 0 and no reliable estimate

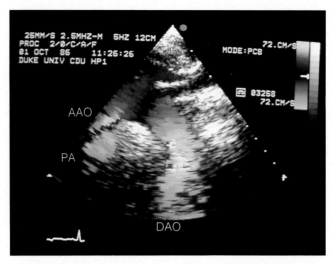

Fig. 6–18. Normal color image from the supersternal notch of the aortic arch. This image contains important information concerning the angular dependency of color flow imaging techniques. The pulmonary artery is seen at the lower left. An enhanced map was used. For details see text.

of flow velocity can be obtained. Thus, even though flow is present it is not displayed and the color appears to move through the black baseline.

Blood moving across the arch and away from the transducer is shifted into blue. As the blood becomes progressively more parallel to the Doppler beam, better estimates of velocity are made and the hues become brighter and brighter. Finally aliasing occurs just at the be-

ginning of the descending aorta where bright blue is shifted into bright yellow. It is here where the best estimate of flow velocity occurs in this image.

Thus, the color flow display is entirely angle-dependent and this dependency is a major limitation of the technique. Those mastering an understanding of this explanation will join Buys Ballot in believing in Doppler and realizing how difficult these principles are to comprehend.

7

Color Flow Imaging of
Valvular Regurgitation

Perhaps the most useful application of color flow imaging is in the detection of valvular regurgitations. Most of the patients we study in our laboratory are examined to determine the presence and relative severity of valvular insufficiency. Color flow techniques avoid the necessity of using the time-consuming pulsed Doppler examination mapping technique and thus reduce patient examination and interpretation times. They do so while providing a spatial display of regurgitant flow.

From this point on, we have made every effort to keep the text at a minimum in order to include as many color flow images as possible. Various points of how to perform and evaluate color flow images for valvular regurgitation and other uses are woven throughout the subsequent discussions.

Mitral Regurgitation

Color flow detection of valvular insufficiencies is relatively easily performed during the course of the routine two-dimensional examination. Almost any view is useful, including the left parasternal long-axis, even though the Doppler beam may be perpendicular, rather than parallel, to flow. Figure 7–1 demonstrates mitral regurgitation directed along the posterior

mitral leaflet toward the posterior left atrial wall. Aliasing is present due to the increased velocity and turbulence through the closed valve orifice and appears as a bright mosaic of colors. When variance detection maps are used they will add green to the regurgitant lesion.

Since abnormal flows within the heart are usually turbulent, many eddy currents exist in literally hundreds of directions simultaneously. Thus, while the main vector of the regurgitant jet may be generally perpendicular to the interrogating beam, there are subsystems of direction as a consequence of these eddies within the main jet that are more parallel to the beam. In most cases, these signals are sufficiently strong to still be detected by the color flow imaging device. Figure 7–2 shows a mitral regurgitant jet directed into the center of the left atrium, nearly perpendicular to the beam. No turbulence map is used, yet the abnormal flow is readily displayed. Note, however, that there is little aliasing present, probably due to the fact that low mean velocity flow estimates were recorded due to relatively perpendicular beam orientation.

Quantitation of the severity of valvular regurgitation is based roughly upon the size and configuration of the regurgitant jet. Very small jets, localized just to the proximal side of the regurgitant valve, usually signify trivial valvular in-

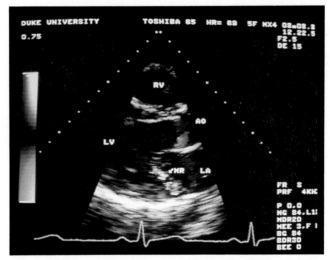

Fig. 7–1. Parasternal long-axis view of mitral regurgitation directed toward the posterior left atrial wall. A turbulence map was used.

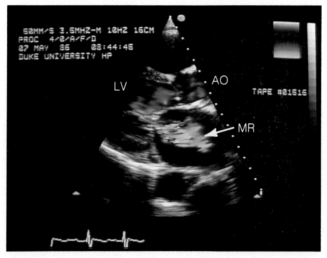

Fig. 7–2. Mitral regurgitation directed into the center of the left atrium. A small degree of aliasing is seen. Presumably the aliasing was reduced because the beam is perpendicular to flow. An enhanced map was used; spatial filters are on. For details see text.

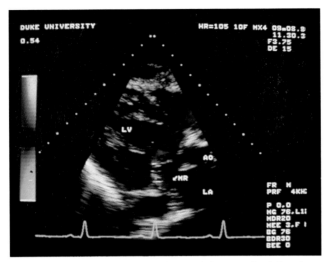

Fig. 7–3. Trivial mitral regurgitation directed toward the posterior left atrium as seen from the parasternal long axis. A turbulence map was used.

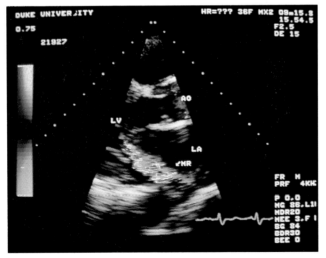

Fig. 7–4. Left parasternal long-axis view showing a more severe degree of mitral regurgitation than seen in Figure 7–3. The jet is again directed against the posterior left atrial wall. A variance map was used.

sufficiency. Large jets that fill the receiving chamber usually signify significant valvular insufficiency. Using these very loose criteria, the mitral regurgitation in Figure 7–1 would be graded mild and that in Figure 7–2 moderate in severity. Figure 7–3 shows a posteriorly directed regurgitant jet that is trivial as detected in the parasternal long axis.

It is imperative to remember that many factors influence the size, configuration and appearance of regurgitant lesions. Amongst them are the volume of the jet, pressure difference between the regurgitant and receiving chamber, size of the regurgitant orifice, configuration of the regurgitant orifice, and size of the receiving chamber. Other factors such as the timing of regurgitation, loading conditions, heart rate, and rhythm may also be of importance. As just mentioned, the orientation of the jet to the beam is also a factor. Considerable work remains in verifying the significance of these and other influences. The reader is directed to current periodical literature for continuing updates on the use of color flow imaging for the quantitation of regurgitant lesions.

Figure 7–4 shows a more severe degree of mitral regurgitation. Again, the hallmark is the systolic appearance of a posteriorly directed jet comprised of aliased colors and turbulence. Regurgitant jets may go in any direction and have virtually any appearance. Figure 7–5 demonstrates mitral regurgitation seen from the subcostal view in a 5-year-old boy in which the jet is more diffuse and occupies almost all of an enlarged left atrium. In this case severe mitral regurgitation is present.

Occasionally, pulmonary venous inflow into the left atrium may be imaged simultaneously with the regurgitant jet. As seen in the moderate to severe regurgitation in Figure 7–6, these atrial flows should not be confused with the regurgitant jet. The pulmonary venous inflow is seen to originate from the posterior wall of the left atrium and is rarely, if ever, aliased. The regurgitant jet is frequently aliased and its origin from the mitral orifice should help to make this differentiation.

Because color flow imaging techniques allow for spatial interrogation of an entire plane of information, the actual regurgitant orifice may sometimes be visualized. Figure 7–7 reveals a large regurgitant orifice through the mitral valve just at the coaptation point. This image is from very early systole; in mid to late systole the entire left atrium filled with regurgitant flow. There is little aliasing here, probably a result of the low pressure difference between the ventricle and atrium in the presence of severe valvular insufficiency. In addition, the interrogating beam is perpendicular to flow resulting in artifactually low mean velocity estimates.

Of course, valves should be interrogated from any possible view to best image a regurgitant jet. Figure 7–8 shows the appearance of a mitral regurgitant jet from the apical four-chamber view. The abnormal pattern is seen originating at the mitral orifice and it moves laterally along the wall of the left atrium to its posterior margin.

Figure 7–9 demonstrates a more centrally positioned jet from the apical four-chamber approach and shows how a pulsed Doppler study may be carried out during a flow imaging examination. A pulsed Doppler sample volume has been located in the center of the severely regurgitant jet and the spectral analysis shown at the left results. This may be helpful in timing certain events but usually is not needed for mapping since the spatial bounds of the abnormality are usually readily identified in the two-dimensional display. Of course, when simultaneous pulse Doppler data is obtained the frame rate of the color flow image must significantly drop or be frozen altogether, to record a reasonable spectral study.

As with the spectral display, a color M-mode may also be displayed. Figure 7–10 shows both the conventional pulsed Doppler spectral display and the color M-mode in the same patient just seen. Aside from exercising the full capability of some color flow devices, there are only rare clinical circumstances when all three need to be displayed at the same time. We have found that it is most convenient to use the simulta-

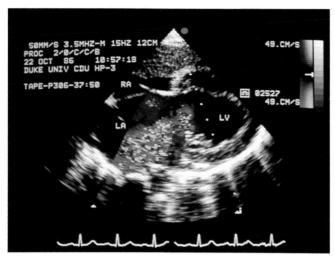

Fig. 7–5. Subcostal view of severe mitral regurgitation. A variance map was used; spatial filters are off.

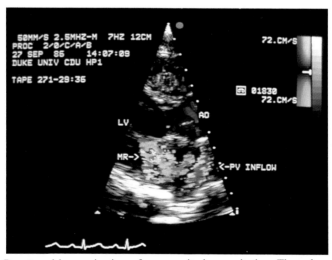

Fig. 7–6. Parasternal long-axis view of severe mitral regurgitation. The pulmonary venous inflow can be seen near the top of the right atrium and should not be confused with the regurgitation jet. A variance map was used.

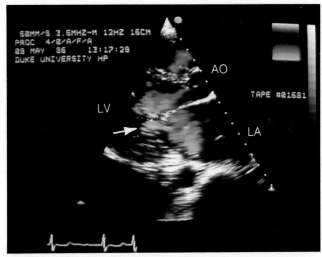

Fig. 7–7. Left parasternal long-axis view of mitral regurgitation. The regurgitant orifice is easily seen (arrow). Little aliasing is present, presumably due to the orientation of the beam. An enhanced map was used; spatial filters are on. For details see text.

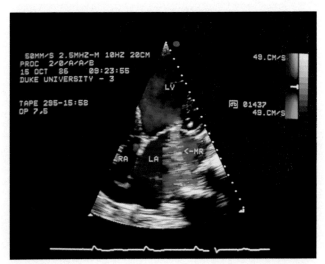

Fig. 7–8. Apical four-chamber view of a mitral regurgitant jet directed toward the lateral wall of the left atrium. A turbulence map was used; spatial filters are on.

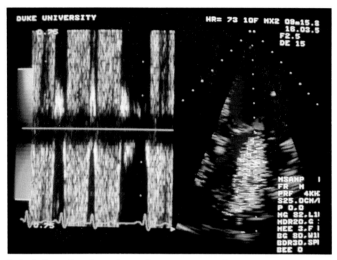

Fig. 7–9. Apical four-chamber view of a more centrally located jet from severe mitral regurgitation. A conventional pulsed Doppler sample volume is located in the central portions of the jet and obscured by the mosaic of regurgitant flow. Conventional spectral analysis appears at left. A variance map was used.

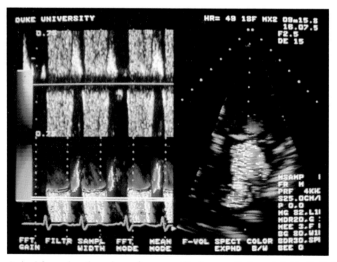

Fig. 7–10. Apical four-chamber view of severe mitral regurgitation at right. Both the spectral pulsed Doppler display and a color M-mode display may be seen. A variance map was used.

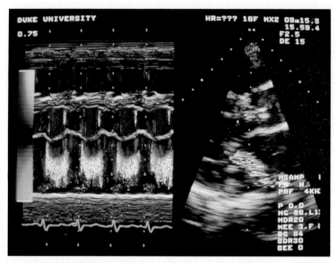

Fig. 7–11. Left parasternal long-axis view of the mitral regurgitant jet seen in the two previous figures. It is directed posteriorly toward the left atrium. Mitral regurgitation is displayed on the M-mode display in systole. A variance map was used.

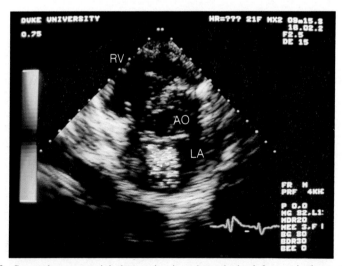

Fig. 7–12. Somewhat tangential short-axis view through the left ventricular outflow tract and left atrium to record further spatial information concerning the mitral regurgitant jet. The patient is the same as in the previous figure. A variance map was used.

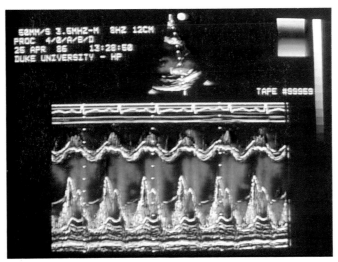

Fig. 7–13. M-mode, color M-mode of mitral regurgitation in a patient with a severe dilated cardiomyopathy.

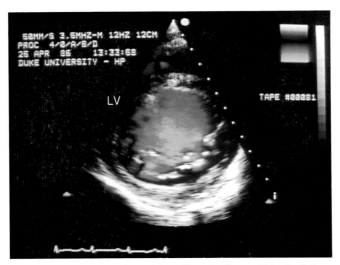

Fig. 7–14. Parasternal short-axis view of late diastolic flow within the left ventricle of a patient with a dilated cardiomyopathy. The low-velocity flow seen in these states is reflected by the less intense colors. An enhanced map was used; spatial filters are on.

neous M-mode display when timing information is desired (Fig. 7–11).

Recording a mitral regurgitant jet in the parasternal short axis gives further spatial location of the abnormality. The user will find that most mitral regurgitant jets are located posteriorly along the back wall of the left atrium as seen in the previous figure. When this occurs, somewhat tangential orientation of the short axis view is required to give better spatial location of the abnormality (Fig. 7–12).

Mitral regurgitation may be found by color flow imaging in the setting of prolapse, rheumatic heart disease, infective endocarditis, or other etiologies. Continued use of color flow imaging has revealed the frequent association of mitral regurgitation (Fig. 7–13) in patients with diffuse cardiomyopathies of virtually any origin. In our laboratory, we have encountered mitral regurgitation in 100 percent of patients with this disorder when the left ventricle measures 6 cm or greater. In each case the mitral regurgitation was quantitated at 2+ or greater (out of a scale of 4). Of further interest is the fact that there is a surprisingly high prevalence of regurgitation of the other heart valves. There is 2+ or greater regurgitation of the tricuspid valve in 91 percent, aortic valve in 23 percent, and the pulmonic valve in 58 percent of patients with dilated cardiomyopathy. In these patients, forward flow is usually of very slow velocity and results in very dull hues of color (Fig. 7–14).

Patients with various forms of cardiomyopathy frequently provide excellent images. Coronary artery flows can occasionally be seen in these settings. Figure 7–15 demonstrates flow in the proximal left main coronary artery and circumflex coronary artery in a patient with a nonobstructive hypertrophic cardiomyopathy. With inferior angulation into the parasternal short-axis view of the left ventricle, flow is seen in the short axis of the left main coronary artery in the same patient (Fig. 7–16).

A number of studies have shown that conventional Doppler techniques are highly specific in the detection of mitral regurgitation. False positive diagnoses have been quite rare when compared to an angiographic standard and specificities as high as 100 percent have been reported. Color flow mapping also appears to be fairly sensitive for detection of mitral regurgitation, though a number of false negatives may occur when compared to cardiac catheterization. In these false negative cases, mitral regurgitation is generally only mild on angiography. In our laboratory we find very favorable correlations between the flow imaging approach and conventional Doppler methods in patients in whom all three methods are performed.

Due to the considerable savings of time, we now exclusively use the color flow approach for the routine detection of valvular insufficiency. This is not done, however, without attending to all the factors that may affect the reliability of our estimation of severity. Operator skill is important. The use of insufficient gain will make regurgitant lesions appear smaller; the use of excessive gain may make a jet appear larger. Proper transducer angulation with respect to the regurgitant lesion is also very important. For small and eccentrically directed jets, extra time is required to be sure of proper identification. Hastily conducted studies limited only to traditional views may not reveal these types of abnormalities.

Aortic Insufficiency

Almost all of the previous comments also apply to the detection and rough quantification of aortic regurgitation. Aortic regurgitant jets may be small and narrow. When they are, location and mapping by conventional pulsed techniques may be very time consuming. Using color flow approaches can readily identify these abnormalities as seen in Figure 7–17. This narrow jet occupied only a very small portion of the area of the outflow tract when viewed in short axis (Fig. 7–18). In both of these views, little aliasing occurs as is sometimes the case from the parasternal approach for reasons described previously.

More typically, a strong turbulent signal is detected and aliasing occurs. Figure 7–19 demonstrates the resultant mosaic across the entire

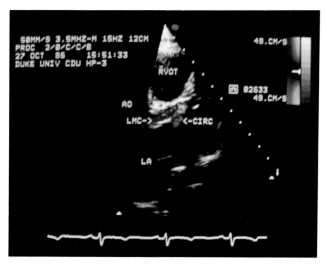

Fig. 7–15. Parasternal short-axis view of flow in the left main coronary artery and proximal circumflex coronary artery from a patient with a nonobstructive hypertrophic cardiomyopathy. Coronary flow may sometimes be seen in these patients. A variance map was used; spatial filters are off.

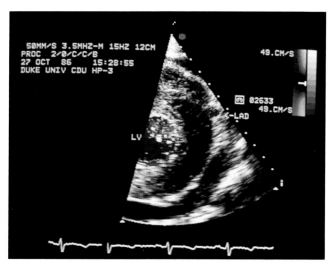

Fig. 7–16. Parasternal short-axis view of the left ventricle in the same patient as seen in Figure 7–15. Note the flow in the short axis of the left anterior descending coronary artery. A variance map was used; spatial filters are off.

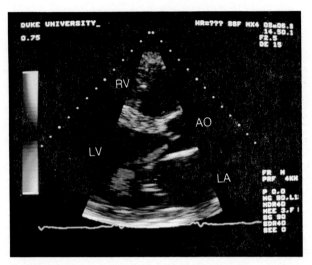

Fig. 7–17. Left parasternal long-axis view of a patient with a very narrow jet of aortic insufficiency. Little aliasing is seen, presumably a result of angular dependency. A variance map was used.

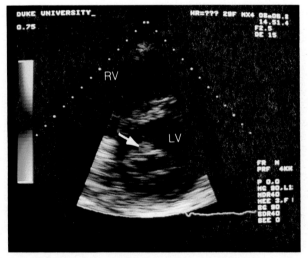

Fig. 7–18. Left parasternal short-axis view of the same regurgitant jet seen in Figure 7–17 (arrow). Location of this jet by conventional means would be most difficult. A variance map was used.

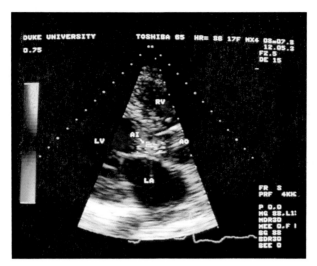

Fig. 7–19. Left parasternal long-axis view of aortic insufficiency filling the entirety of the left ventricular outflow tract in diastole. The mosaic of the moderate aortic regurgitation is easily recognized. A variance map was used.

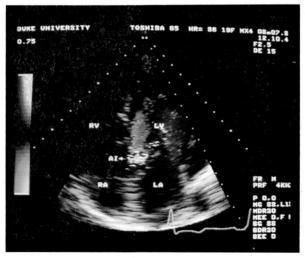

Fig. 7–20. Apical four-chamber view from the same patient as seen in Figure 7–19. Left ventricular inflow can be seen in dull hues of red. Mosaic of aortic insufficiency is easily recognized in late diastole. A variance map was used.

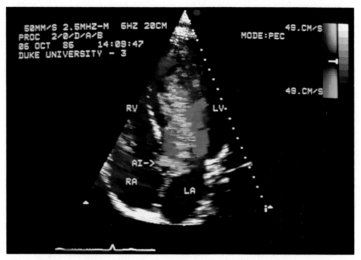

Fig. 7–21. Apical four-chamber view of severe aortic insufficiency. Note the mosaic of color extending from the aortic valve to the apex of the left ventricle. A variance map was used; spatial filters are on.

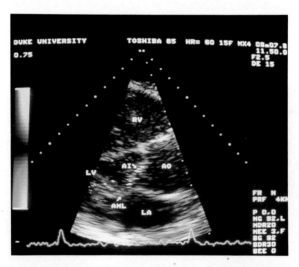

Fig. 7–22. Parasternal long-axis view of a narrow aortic regurgitant jet directed at the anterior mitral valve leaflet. This jet seems to bounce off the leaflet toward the left. This type of aortic regurgitation frequently accounts for the origin of an Austin-Flint murmur. A variance map was used.

left ventricular outflow tract in diastole resulting from aortic insufficiency. The area of the jet can be further identified using the apical approach (Fig. 7–20).

When aortic regurgitation is severe, more of the left ventricle fills in diastole. Figure 7–21 shows severe aortic insufficiency from the apical four-chamber view where virtually all of the left ventricle is filled with aliasing and turbulence. Interestingly, this patient remains asymp-

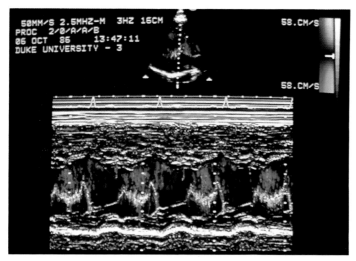

Fig. 7–23. Color M-mode tracing of rapid oscillations of an anterior mitral valve leaflet from a patient with severe aortic insufficiency. Because of the rapid oscillations color is recorded along the mitral valve leaflet. A variance map was used. For details see text.

tomatic despite the significant hemodynamic load.

The various directions of flow resulting from aortic insufficiency also reveal useful information other than presence or severity alone. Figure 7–22 demonstrates an aortic regurgitant jet directed toward the anterior mitral valve leaflet then reflected off to the left in a patient with a low pitched diastolic rumbling murmur suggestive of mitral stenosis. No aortic insufficiency murmur was audible. No mitral stenosis was present by echo or Doppler. Even though the degree of aortic insufficiency was small, the direction of the jet readily explained the origin of the murmur as it was likely that the regurgitant jet set the mitral valve into rapid vibrations. This is the classical description of the origin of the Austin-Flint mitral rumble.

When the aortic jet is so directed or the degree of insufficiency is so large, it may cause the mitral valve leaflet to move so rapidly that no amount of wall filtering can eliminate color from the leaflet itself. This is readily seen in Figure 7–23 in a patient with severe aortic insufficiency. More typically, smaller jets directed toward the anterior mitral leaflet are seen on M-mode just anterior to the leaflet and fail to

establish a resonance on the leaflet that appears on the color display (Fig. 7–24).

In some patients, the precise point of aortic insufficiency may be located in the parasternal short-axis view of the aortic valve. Figure 7–25 reveals that the aortic insufficiency in this patient is between the coaptation point of the left and noncoronary cusps.

Many of these potential uses are brought together in review of a case of a 30-year-old patient with mild fevers and two positive blood cultures several months prior to admission. The patient was treated with antibiotics for several weeks at an outside hospital. The patient had increasing dyspnea and was admitted to Duke severely short of breath with a clinical diagnosis of aortic insufficiency. His color flow studies are seen in Figures 7–26 through 7–29.

Initial long-axis study revealed a large and markedly turbulent aortic insufficiency jet from the valve plane directed toward the apex of the left ventricle along the posterior aspect of the interventricular septum (Fig. 7–26). Of great interest was the fact that the onset of mitral insufficiency occurred in late diastole and before the onset of mechanical systole (Fig. 7–27). Thus both valves were regurgitant at the same

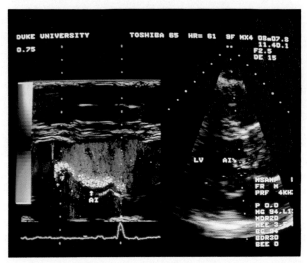

Fig. 7–24. Mild aortic insufficiency directed toward the anterior mitral valve leaflet is seen at the right. Usually, the jet from the aortic insufficiency is readily differentiated from the mitral valve leaflet seen at left on the color M-mode. A variance map was used.

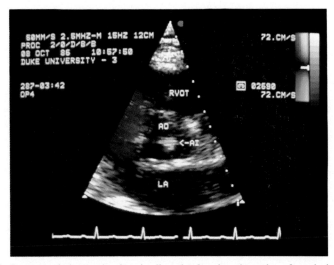

Fig. 7–25. Parasternal short-axis view in diastole showing the point of aortic insufficiency between the left and noncoronary cusps. A variance map was used; spatial filters are on.

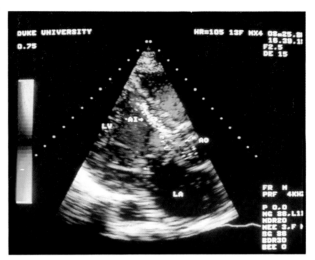

Fig. 7–26. Parasternal long-axis view of severe aortic insufficiency following the posterior portion of the interventricular septum. A variance map was used. This is the same patient as shown in Figures 7–27, 7–28, and 7–29.

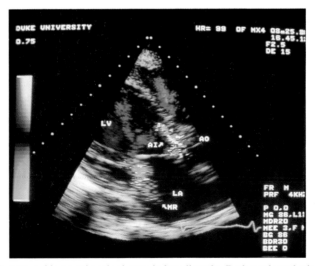

Fig. 7–27. Parasternal long-axis color image in late diastole. Both aortic and mitral regurgitations are seen simultaneously. This patient has acute aortic insufficiency and is the same patient as shown in Figure 7–26. A variance map was used.

time. The left ventricle was judged to be mildly dilated and diffusely hypocontractile.

With the M-mode beam directed through the mitral valve and both regurgitant jets, premature closure of the mitral valve apparatus was noted to occur well before the QRS complex as a likely result of the significant hemodynamic load of the aortic insufficiency (Fig. 7–28). The left ventricular diastolic pressure was high enough to close the mitral valve before the onset of systole. Of note is the fact that most of the mitral regurgitation was seen before mechanical systole began; following the QRS complex, little mitral regurgitation was noted. It was presumed that if the hemodynamic load of aortic insufficiency could be reduced and the timing of mitral valve closure returned to normal there was little likelihood that significant mitral regurgitation would be left. Of additional interest, diastolic short-axis images of the aortic valve revealed that this torrential aortic insufficiency was emerging into the left ventricle through the area of the left coronary cusp (Fig. 7–29).

These data delivered important information by which to guide the surgical approach. First, the aortic insufficiency was, indeed, severe. Second, the hemodynamic load upon the left ventricle was significant and caused premature closure of the mitral valve. Both of these factors indicated that immediate aortic valve replacement was necessary. Third, since almost all of the mitral regurgitation was during the latter part of diastole, correction of the aortic insufficiency was likely to reduce or eliminate the degree of mitral regurgitation. No replacement of the mitral apparatus was likely necessary.

On the basis of the patient's deteriorating condition and these data alone, the patient underwent aortic valve replacement without catheterization. A 6-mm-diameter hole was seen through the left coronary cusp. No vegetations were seen on the mitral apparatus. Postoperatively the patient was left with trivial mitral regurgitation.

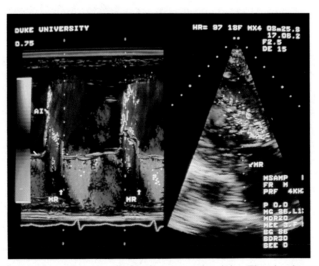

Fig. 7–28. The severe aortic regurgitation is seen at the right. The simultaneous M-mode color recording shows premature closure of the mitral valve apparatus and the onset of mitral regurgitation in mid to late diastole. Note that the mitral regurgitation is reduced after mechanical systole begins. This is the same patient as shown in Figures 7–26 and 7–27. A variance map was used.

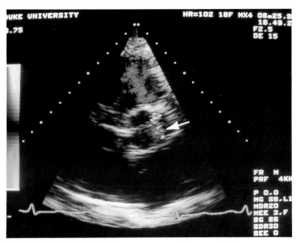

Fig. 7–29. Left parasternal short-axis view of the aortic valve cusps in the same patient shown in Figures 7–26 through 7–28. Almost the entirety of the left coronary cusp is seen to fill with color in diastole indicating the location of the regurgitant orifice (arrow). A variance map was used.

Tricuspid Regurgitation

Regurgitation of the tricuspid valve, like all the other cardiac valves, is best detected during the two-dimensional echocardiographic examination. The most common views in which tricuspid insufficiency is detected are the apical four-chamber view, short-axis parasternal view at the level of the aortic root, subcostal view, and the right ventricular inlet view. Figure 7–30 shows a tricuspid insufficiency jet filling well over half of the right atrial cavity.

As with the other valves, tricuspid regurgitant jets may be found in any size, spatial configuration, and direction. Figure 7–31 demonstrates a longer and narrower jet of tricuspid regurgitation that nearly reaches the posterior wall of the right atrium. It appears directed toward the interatrial septum.

Tricuspid regurgitation is frequently found, even in normal patients. In these cases, the area of the regurgitation is usually small. Little is known about the sensitivity and specificity of color flow in detection of this lesion since there are no gold standards available for comparison. Angiography requires that a catheter be placed across the tricuspid valve; such catheter placement may itself create valvular regurgitation. Tricuspid regurgitation is found with the same prevalence with color flow Doppler as with conventional Doppler methods.

Tricuspid regurgitant jets, like all the others, may be of any size and directed at any angle. Figure 7–32 demonstrates a small jet angled toward the interatrial septum from the apical four-chamber approach. The jet may be noted to move from one side of the atrium to the other during the course of systole.

Regurgitant jets may not be symmetric when imaged in orthogonal views. Figure 7–33 shows a jet of tricuspid insufficiency as seen from the left parasternal short axis view. It is quite different in proportion and configuration when imaged from a modified apical four-chamber view (Fig. 7–34).

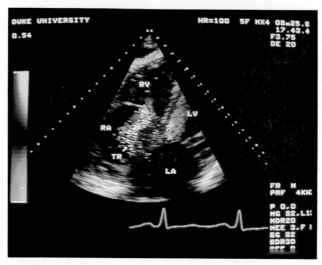

Fig. 7–30. Modified apical four-chamber view of severe tricuspid regurgitation. A variance map was used.

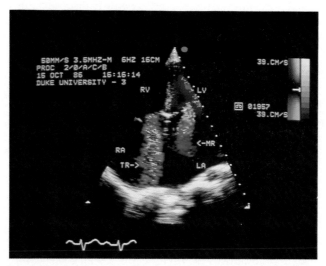

Fig. 7–31. Apical four-chamber view of both tricuspid and mitral regurgitations. The tricuspid regurgitant jet is directed toward the interatrial septum. A variance map was used; spatial filters are off.

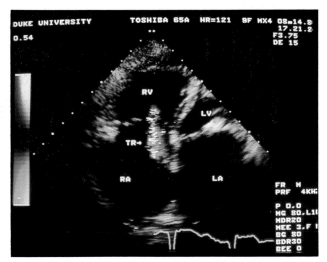

Fig. 7–32. Modified apical four-chamber view of a small tricuspid regurgitant jet directed toward the interatrial septum. A variance map was used.

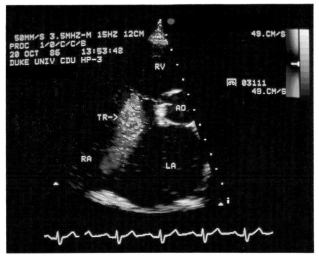

Fig. 7–33. Parasternal short-axis view of the aorta showing one configuration of a tricuspid regurgitation jet. A variance map was used; spatial filters are off.

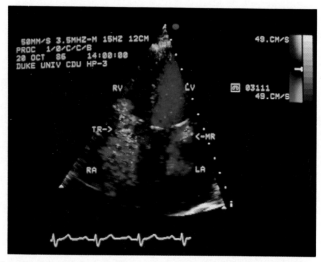

Fig. 7–34. Modified apical four-chamber view of the same jet seen in the previous figure. It is quite different in appearance. See text for details. A variance map was used; spatial filters are off.

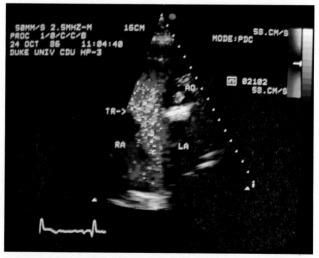

Fig. 7–35. Parasternal short-axis view of tricuspid regurgitation with marked turbulence at the level of the closed tricuspid valve. The jet tapers as it approaches the interatrial septum. A variance map was used; spatial filters are off.

Other appearances of tricuspid regurgitation are possible. Figure 7–35 shows marked turbulence at the level of the closed tricuspid valve with a jet tapering in size toward the interatrial septum. This patient had severe, clinical tricus-pid regurgitation. When severe, the jet can be seen to fill the right atrium.

M-mode color flow of tricuspid regurgitation can also be performed. From the apical four-chamber approach it appears as a burst of color

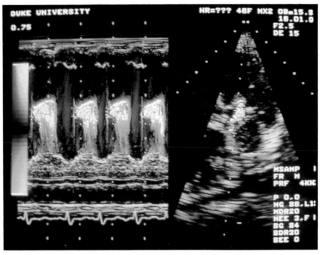

Fig. 7–36. Modified apical four-chamber view of tricuspid regurgitation with accompanying M-mode display. A variance map was used.

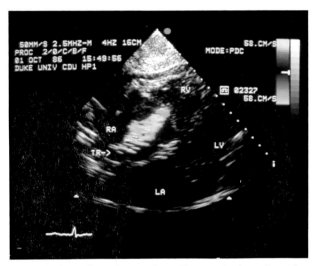

Fig. 7–37. Subcostal view of moderate tricuspid regurgitation. An enhanced map was used; spatial filters are on.

away from the transducer during systole as seen in Figure 7–36. When the apical four-chamber view is of marginal or poor quality, it is occasionally necessary to place the transducer into the subcostal position and angle superiorly to record the regurgitant flow. Figure 7–37 shows such a regurgitant lesion. In these cases, however, the interrogating beam is usually relatively perpendicular to flow and the mosaic of aliasing may be absent as a result.

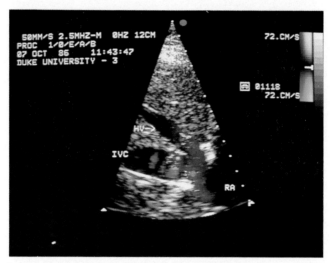

Fig. 7–38. Long-axis view of the inferior vena cava during systole where tricuspid regurgitant flow is shown in red. Note the regurgitant flow into the hepatic vein. A variance map was used; spatial filters are on.

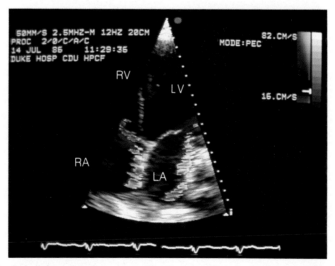

Fig. 7–39. Apical four-chamber view of both tricuspid and mitral regurgitations. The jets are directed toward the right in each case. A variance map with baseline shift was used, and little aliasing is displayed.

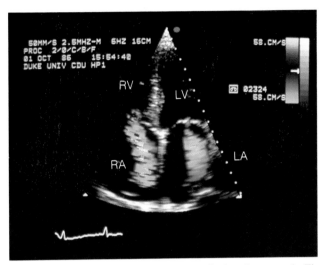

Fig. 7–40. Slightly greater tricuspid and mitral regurgitation than seen in Figure 7–39 are present. An enhanced map was used; spatial filters are on. Slight aliasing can be seen.

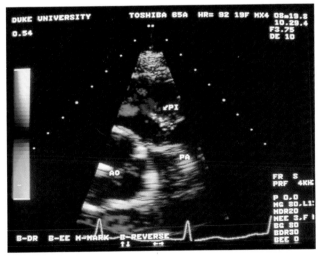

Fig. 7–41. A flame-like appearance of pulmonic insufficiency is seen in the left parasternal short axis view. A turbulence map was used.

When it is necessary to assess tricuspid regurgitation and transthoracic and subcostal approaches are unrewarding, examination of the hepatic veins and inferior vena cava is frequently helpful. In systole, a reversal of color in comparison to diastole may be recorded when tricuspid insufficiency is present. Figure 7–38 reveals such reversal of flow.

In most cases, however, regurgitation through the tricuspid valve is readily detected from the apex. An operator should always be aware that mitral regurgitation may be detected from the same view. Figure 7–39 shows both mitral and tricuspid regurgitations coexisting in the same patient. The regurgitation through the tricuspid valve is directed along the interatrial septum while that from the mitral valve is directed along the lateral wall of the left atrium. In this image, the baseline has been shifted and has removed the aliasing frequently seen in regurgitant flows.

Figure 7–40 is an apical four-chamber view from another patient with coexisting atrioventricular valve regurgitations. In this case there are similar but slightly different directions of regurgitations. The baseline is in the center and aliasing is displayed in both.

Pulmonic Insufficiency

Color flow detection of pulmonary insufficiency is also possible. The most common view in which this lesion can be obtained is the left parasternal short axis view. A flame-like regurgitant jet is seen in the right ventricular outflow tract in diastole. An operator may need to angle the beam to open the right ventricular outflow tract more fully to detect and appropriately record small degrees of this disorder. Figure 7–41 shows the typical appearance of moderate pulmonary insufficiency. In patients with mild pulmonary insufficiency just a small bit of color is seen at or near the coaptation point of the pulmonic cusps. When the entirety of the right ventricular outflow tract is filled with color, the degree of pulmonary insufficiency is severe.

8

Color Flow Imaging of Valvular Stenosis

Doppler color flow imaging methods allow for identification of the presence of certain valvular stenotic jets. There are no, however, specific characteristics in the color display of stenotic flows that assist in quantitating the severity of valvular obstruction at the present time. Spatial location of the direction of a jet is possible and this may be used to direct a continuous-wave conventional Doppler beam at an optimum angle to flow for precise measurement of peak velocity data. Details of the use of peak velocity information for estimating transvalvular gradients or valve areas are based upon the modified Bernoulli equation and readers are referred to any standard conventional Doppler textbook for discussions of this very useful application.

Mitral Stenosis

Mitral stenotic jets are characterized by a bright burst of color from the mitral valve orifice in very early diastole as seen in Figure 8–1A, where the jet is imaged in the apical four-chamber approach. An instant later, a central core of aliasing is frequently seen that persists throughout the remainder of diastole (Fig. 8–1B). This appearance has often been referred to as the ''flame-like'' pattern of mitral stenosis and is present in many, but not all, patients with mitral stenosis.

The apical views are clearly the best for recording this characteristic appearance as the interrogating beam is nearly parallel to flow and the best mean velocity estimates are possible. Figure 8–2 shows a typical mitral stenotic jet from the apical four-chamber view. Note that a central core of aliasing is less evident in this jet.

In a very high number of cases, the mitral stenotic jet is directed toward the apex of the left ventricle. Such a jet is seen in the patient in Figure 8–3. Here the mitral inflow jet is nearly parallel to the interventricular septum when viewed from the apical two-chamber view. This is not always true, however, and these jets may be oriented in any direction as a function of the size and configuration of the orifice itself. Figure 8–4 shows a mitral stenotic jet that actually bifurcates. Jets of two directions, one toward the interventricular septum and the other toward the ventricular apex, are visualized in this left parasternal long-axis view.

In these figures, there is an area of color on the atrial side of the stenotic valve leaflets. This area of increased blood cell velocity results in intense coloration in this area and presumably results from the red blood cells becoming ordered before entering the stenotic valve orifice.

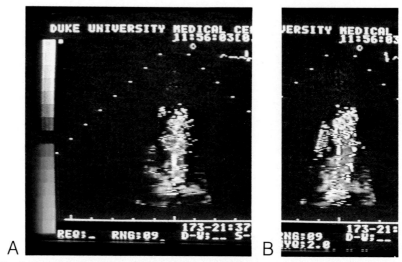

Fig. 8–1. (A) Apical four-chamber view of a mitral stenotic jet in early diastole. During this phase, most mitral stenotic jets appear of uniform color. (B) An instant later, a central core of aliasing is frequently seen that persists throughout the remainder of diastole. A variance map was used.

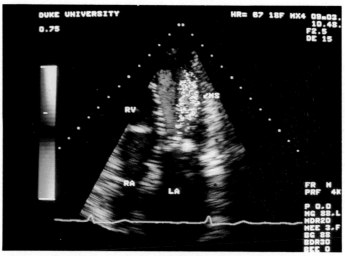

Fig. 8–2. Apical four-chamber view demonstrating that most mitral stenotic jets are directed toward the apex of the left ventricle. A variance map was used.

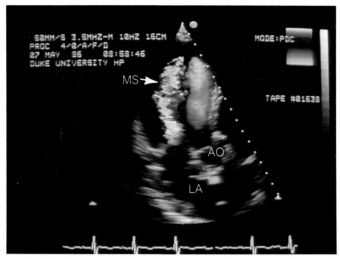

Fig. 8–3. Apical two-chamber view of a mitral stenotic jet easily separated from the normal flow in the left ventricular outflow tract adjacent to the septum. An enhanced map was used; spatial filters are on.

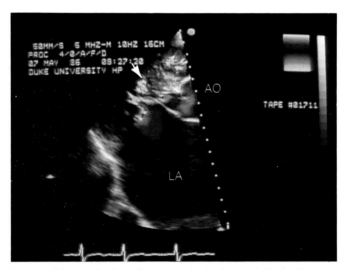

Fig. 8–4. Parasternal long-axis view of an unusual mitral stenotic jet that is seen to bifurcate. One portion of the jet is directed toward the apex and the other toward the interventricular septum (arrow). Note the color on the atrial side of the mitral valve leaflet that is characteristic of mild turbulence in the prestenotic area. An enhanced map was used; spatial filters are on.

Frequently quite large in patients with severe mitral stenosis (as seen in Fig. 8–4), this area usually becomes smaller as diastole persists and is usually quite small at the end of diastole.

While this area of somewhat disturbed flow is nearly always seen in mitral stenosis, it is not specific for this disorder. Figure 8–5 demonstrates a large area of disturbed diastolic flow within the left atrium and then through the mitral orifice in a patient with Libman-Sachs endocarditis. In this patient the posterior mitral valve leaflet was quite thickened and immobile, resulting in an area of turbulent flow. No mitral stenosis was noted with conventional Doppler methods.

This area has also been noted in some instances of mitral regurgitation and is presumed due to high volume flow passing through the mitral valve in early diastole. It is also seen in hypertrophic cardiomyopathy, possibly a consequence of poor left ventricular compliance and an impairment in diastolic filling. However, when noted in disorders other than mitral stenosis, the pattern appears only briefly, in very early diastole.

To date, several attempts to quantitate the severity of mitral stenois by assessing diastolic jet area or other characteristics have been unsuccessful. Similarly, neither the size nor the appearance of the prestenotic jet has been noted to be helpful for quantitative purposes.

With significant mitral stenosis the transmitral pressure gradient remains elevated throughout diastole and mitral inflow velocities will decrease slowly. The area of prestenotic coloration will persist until late diastole in this setting. This color flow equivalent of a prolonged pressure half-time on the continuous-wave Doppler is not very helpful for precise quantitative purposes, however. Thus, while the appearance of mitral stenosis is very characteristic, little useful information for quantitating severity has been identified to date by color flow imaging.

When a color imaging system contains continuous-wave Doppler capabilities, identification of the direction of the stenotic jet is very helpful and allows for reasonably precise parallel orientation of a continuous-wave beam with the stenotic jet. This provides a means for operator interaction, assuring orientation of the beam as close to parallel to flow as possible.

The image in Figure 8–6 shows a color flow

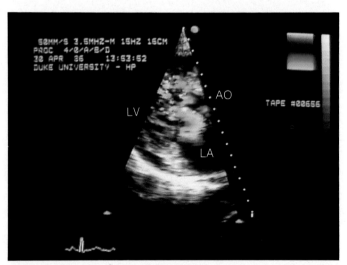

Fig. 8–5. Parasternal long-axis view of turbulence seen through the mitral valve orifice of a patient with Libman-Sachs endocarditis. No mitral valve obstruction was noted on conventional Doppler. An enhanced map was used.

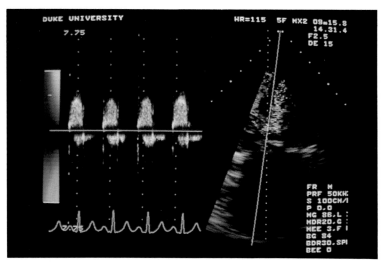

Fig. 8–6. Color flow imaging may be used to direct a continuous-wave beam through the mitral stenotic jet. At the right is a color flow image from the apical four-chamber view where a continuous-wave beam (dotted line) is directed toward the mitral valve orifice. The beam is not perfectly aligned with the jet. At the left is the continuous-wave spectral velocity recording. A turbulence map was used.

image in which a continuous-wave beam (dotted line) was directed toward the stenotic jet (right). In this system the focal point of the continuous-wave Doppler may be varied. Where the solid line intersects the dotted line is the focal point. Note that the interrogating beam intercepts the jet near its origin and the remainder of the jet moves off to the right. This creates a considerable angle between beam and direction of flow and renders the measurement of peak velocity less reliable than it would be with perfectly parallel direction. When this situation is encountered, the operator must try other minor angulations to ensure that the continuous-wave beam is as parallel to flow as possible. Several studies have shown that color flow guided estimates of peak velocities in mitral stenosis are superior to those performed blindly.

Figure 8–7 shows the proper beam orientation for recording peak velocity data from a patient with mild mitral stenosis and a peak transmitral valve gradient of 2 m/sec. Figure 8–8 demonstrates the combined use of color flow and continuous-wave Doppler for detection of more se-

vere stenosis where the peak transmitral valve gradient approaches 3 m/sec. The pressure half-time is also markedly delayed in this patient. When using systems equipped with continuous-wave capabilities, the color flow image is automatically frozen when switching into the conventional mode.

With conventional Doppler approaches it is sometimes difficult for beginners to readily separate and distinguish the jet of mitral stenosis from that of aortic insufficiency. This may lead to overestimation of the size of the aortic regurgitant jet using conventional pulsed Doppler mapping techniques. Color flow imaging illustrates the means by which this overestimation might occur. Figure 8–9 demonstrates the blending of an aortic insufficiency jet with that of mitral stenosis from the apical two-chamber view. Here the aortic insufficiency follows the course of the thickened anterior mitral valve leaflet and combines with the mitral stenotic flow.

Color flow imaging usually separates these two jets quite readily. Figure 8–10 shows how

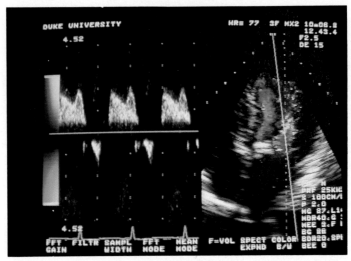

Fig. 8–7. Here, the continuous-wave beam (dotted line) is aligned with the mitral stenotic jet in a more parallel fashion. In these cases, the spectral recording of peak velocity would be more reliable (at left). A variance map was used.

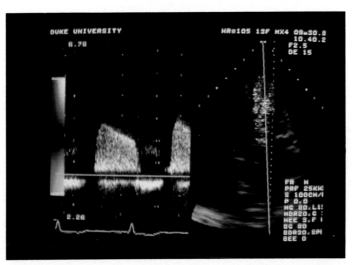

Fig. 8–8. More severe mitral stenosis is depicted on the spectral recording at left. For details see text. A variance map was used.

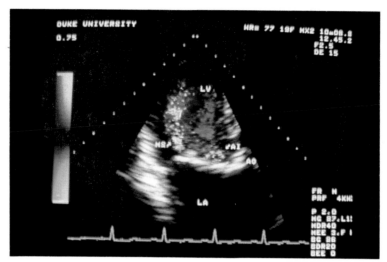

Fig. 8–9. An apical two-chamber view of an aortic insufficiency jet merging with one from mitral stenosis. This frequently results in difficulties in distinguishing the two jets by conventional Doppler means. For details see text. A variance map was used.

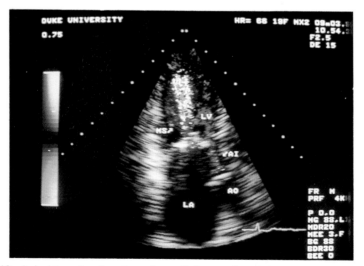

Fig. 8–10. Apical two-chamber view of a small degree of aortic insufficiency readily distinguished from that of mitral stenosis. A variance map was used.

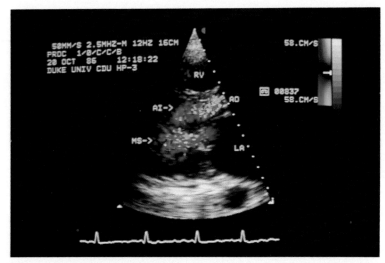

Fig. 8–11. Parasternal long-axis view of severe aortic insufficiency that is readily distinguished from that of mitral stenosis. A variance map was used; spatial filters are off.

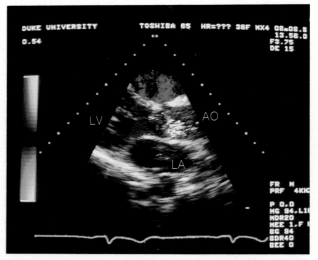

Fig. 8–12. Parasternal long-axis view of a diffuse jet of aortic stenosis. It is quite difficult to obtain directional information from color flow Doppler in aortic stenosis. A variance map was used.

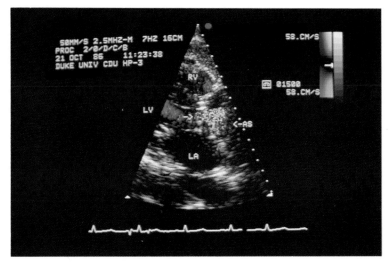

Fig. 8–13. Parasternal long-axis jet of aortic stenosis. Marked turbulence is seen when these jets can be detected that originate at the aortic valve level (arrow) and are seen to fill almost the entirety of the aortic root. A variance map was used.

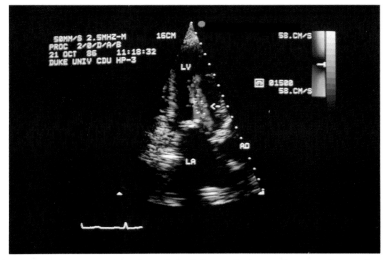

Fig. 8–14. Apical two-chamber view of the left ventricular outflow tract in a patient with aortic stenosis. Flow is occasionally seen to "line-up" prior to entering the stenotic orifice (arrow). Note that no turbulence is visualized in the aorta. A variance map was used; spatial filters are off.

a minor degree of aortic regurgitation is separated from mitral stenosis from the apical two-chamber view. A larger degree of aortic insufficiency is easily distinguished from mitral stenosis in the patient imaged in Figure 8–11 in the left parasternal long-axis approach.

Aortic Stenosis

Unlike mitral stenosis, the forward jet of aortic stenosis into the aortic root is rarely well delineated using color flow methods. Figure 8–12 demonstrates a parasternal long axis view in a patient showing a poorly circumscribed aortic jet that is composed of a diffuse mosaic. In this disorder turbulence is seen to fill almost the entirety of the aortic root and possess little directional information. When imaged, these jets frequently have marked variance in the final display as is seen in Figure 8–13. Note that the turbulence begins at the orifice (arrow) and generally fills the entirety of the root. In most cases, the jet is less well visualized.

Little is known about why it is so difficult to detect an aortic stenotic jet. It is possible that fibrotic and/or calcific changes present in a chronically thickened aortic valve result in attenuation and/or reverberations that obscure the jet flow. It is also possible that energy from the high-velocity aortic jet is so rapidly dissipated that signal-to-noise ratios present in most color flow systems fail to separate the jet from background noise. Whatever the case, using color flow imaging to assist in orientation of a continuous-wave Doppler beam to obtain the most reliable measurement of peak systolic aortic velocity is rarely, if ever, possible using current systems. In most cases, it is quite difficult to detect any turbulence above the level of the diseased aortic valve cusps.

It is, however, frequently possible to visualize systolic flow in the left ventricular outflow tract, just before blood exits through the aortic valve orifice. Flow in the left ventricular outflow tract takes the form of a narrowed jet, as if the red cells were "lining up" to pass through the narrowed aortic valve. This may be seen in almost any view. Figure 8–14 shows this area from an apical two chamber view. Note that the systolic jet in the aorta is poorly visualized. This pattern is quite distinctive and contrasts markedly with the pattern of left ventricular outflow seen in normals where flow almost always fills the entire width of the outflow tract.

Dynamic subvalvular stenosis as is seen in hypertrophic obstructive cardiomyopathy may also have changes noted by color flow imaging. In this disorder, also known as idiopathic hypertrophic subaortic stenosis, systolic anterior motion of the mitral leaflet is thought to occur as a consequence of high-velocity flow through a left ventricular outflow tract narrowed by septal hypertrophy. Venturi forces resulting from this high-velocity flow then pull the mitral leaflet up, toward the septum. These events may lead to incompetence of the mitral valve during systole and result in mitral insufficiency in many patients with this disorder.

Subvalvular obstruction in this disorder results in an area of high velocity and turbulence as seen in Figure 8–15. Most frequently, an area of aliasing in systole results just at the tip of the anterior mitral valve leaflet. In normal individuals, such subvalvular aliasing is rarely, if ever, seen in this region using a 2.5-MHz transducer.

Color M-mode is frequently helpful in this setting as it allows for more precise timing of events. Figure 8–16 demonstrates the onset of aliasing (as a consequence of obstruction) well after the closure of the mitral valve and persisting through the entirety of mid systole. When no obstruction is present, no such aliasing and turbulence are seen.

As noted, patients with this disorder frequently have mitral regurgitation as a result of the geometry of mitral leaflet coaptation. Figure 8–17 shows a parasternal long axis in systole from another patient with hypertrophic obstructive cardiomyopathy. Note that the systolic turbulence mosaic begins near the tip of the mitral

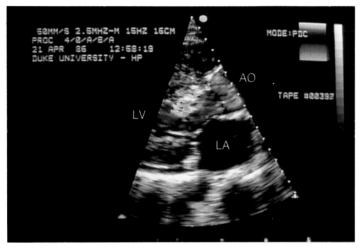

Fig. 8–15. Left parasternal long-axis view from a patient with hypertrophic obstructive cardiomyopathy. Note the aliasing seen in the left ventricular outflow tract. For details see text. An enhanced map was used; spatial filters are on.

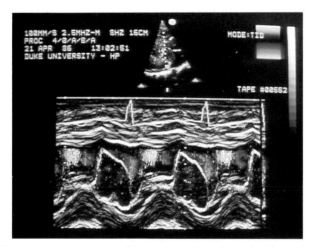

Fig. 8–16. M-mode echocardiogram of the same patient shown in Figure 8–15. Note the area of aliasing in the left ventricular outflow tract in systole. An enhanced map was used.

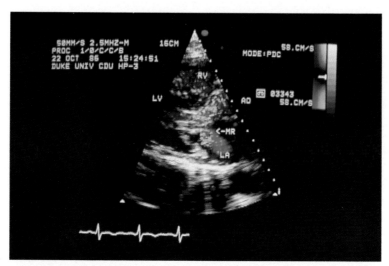

Fig. 8–17. Left parasternal long-axis view systolic frame from another patient with hypertrophic obstructive cardiomyopathy. Turbulence begins at the left ventricular outflow tract level and extends into the aortic root. Mitral regurgitation is coexistent. A variance map was used; spatial filters are off.

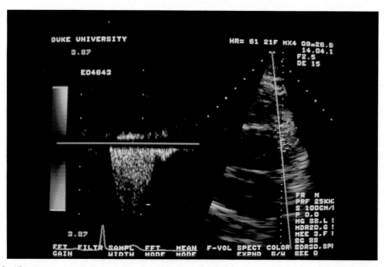

Fig. 8–18. Parasternal short-axis view of the aortic root with the continuous-wave Doppler beam (dotted line) directed through a jet of pulmonary stenosis. This approach may be utilized for detecting peak velocity information from continuous-wave Doppler. A variance map was used.

valve leaflets and extends into the left ventricular outflow tract. Mitral regurgitation is coexistent.

Tricuspid Stenosis

Tricuspid stenosis results in a color flow imaging study very similar to that of mitral stenosis except that the abnormal flow is seen to emerge from the tethered tricuspid valve leaflets. Tricuspid stenosis is encountered rarely and, as a consequence, may not be considered as a diagnostic possibility. It may be missed on an M-mode, two-dimensional, or conventional Doppler examination if the tricuspid valve is not properly interrogated. The spatial display of information on the color flow approach results in the characteristic flame-like jet through the tricuspid valve that readily calls attention to this disorder. As with all the other cardiac valves, there is no useful information in the color flow display to assess severity of the disorder and conventional pulsed or continuous-wave methods must be utilized to derive pressure gradients from the peak velocity data. The characteristic jet is frequently helpful in directing a continuous-wave Doppler beam for more accurate assessment of the degree of valvular stenosis.

Pulmonic Stenosis

Stenosis of the pulmonary valve usually results in a very diffuse jet like that of aortic stenosis. It is, however, more readily detected than that of aortic stenosis. Most degrees of pulmonary stenosis fill the proximal pulmonary artery with a large mosaic, resulting from the aliasing and turbulence as is seen in Figure 8–18. This mosaic is not very specific, however, as similar turbulence may be encountered in patients with ductus arteriosus or as a result from cardiac shunts elsewhere in the heart that result in very high pulmonary flows. In any event, the jet is so diffusely directed that it is not helpful in directing a continuous-wave beam. The diagnosis of pulmonic stenosis should not be established by color flow imaging alone and requires the additional use of conventional means for more specificity. This figure illustrates the continuous-wave beam through the diffuse mosaic.

9

Color Flow Imaging of
Prosthetic Valves

Imaging of flow through prosthetic valves is possible and may be of great help in assessing the proper working status of these valves. Since color flow imaging is so successful in detecting insufficiency from native valves, it might simply be assumed that it is as useful for assessment of prosthetic valve dysfunction. Given an understanding of certain limitations of ultrasound, prosthetic valvular function can be assessed to a highly useful degree.

The Concept of Flow Masking

Once emitted from the transducer into the tissues, ultrasound is either reflected, attenuated (absorbed), or continues on to another tissue interface where the process is repeated. All prosthetic valves contain some degree of nonbiologic material which may be some sort of plastic, metal or cloth. Each of these materials may have highly reflective or attenuative properties that may not allow the ultrasound to penetrate and pass through the nonbiologic portion of the valve.

This nonbiologic material may interfere with the transmission of sound waves to such a degree that it may be impossible to detect some valvular regurgitation. To demonstrate this point, we review an experiment performed some time ago during our initial experiences with Doppler color flow techniques.

A 100-gallon water tank was filled with water and let stand for several days to allow all dissolved gas to come out of solution. A motor pump was attached to tubing filled with a solution of tiny plastic particles to serve as strong Doppler reflectors (Fig. 9–1). The tubing was then suspended diagonally in the water tank and the fluid circulated at a velocity of 6 m/sec. A color flow transducer was suspended just under the water line and the interrogating plane directed toward the diagonal tubing where flow was readily detected. Various cardiac valves were then alternately placed on a small stage constructed of nylon fishing line and suspended from an arm extending from a ring stand with the stage at a range of approximately 10 cm from the face of the transducer.

This assembly provided a means for imitating the spatial position of a mitral prosthetic valve with the transducer at the apex. The flow through the tubing could simulate turbulent flow of mitral regurgitation within the left atrium behind the valve. With no valve in place the flow within the tubing was readily visualized (Fig. 9–2).

With the transducer and tubing fixed in place, six different heart valves were alternately placed on the stage: Starr-Edwards (Silastic ball),

127

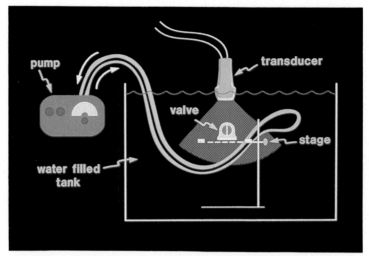

Fig. 9–1. Schematic diagram of an experimental assembly for the study of prosthetic valve flow masking. For details, see text.

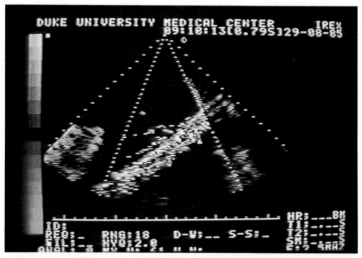

Fig. 9–2. Color flow image through the tubing in the experimental assembly with no prosthetic valve in place. Flow was easily detected during the control periods. A variance map was used.

Starr-Edwards (stellite ball), Bjork-Shiley, St. Jude's, Hall-Kastor, and a porcine bioprosthesis. All valves are shown in Figure 9–3. When placed on the stage, all were in the fully closed position.

What is quite remarkable is that all of the cardiac prosthetic valves have a characteristic shadow, or mask, on the flow behind them. Figure 9–4 shows the masks from all the valves, which indicate a general inability of the ultra-

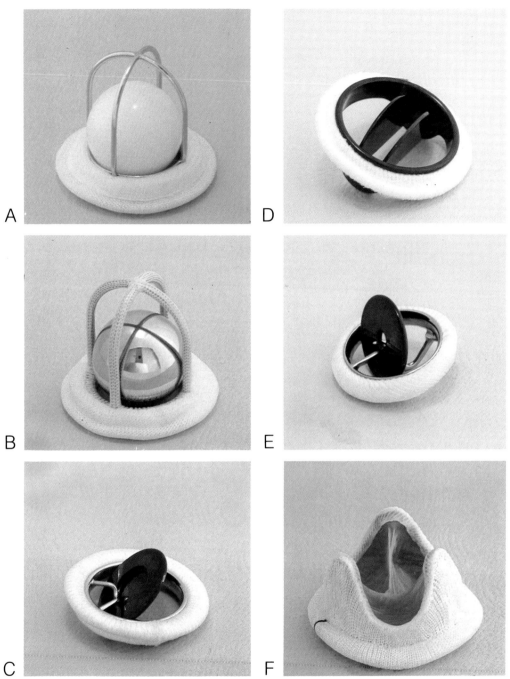

Fig. 9–3. Composite photographs of six different prosthethic heart valves. **(A)** Starr-Edwards Silastic ball valve; **(B)** Starr-Edwards stellite ball valve; **(C)** Bjork-Shiley tilting disk valve in the open position; **(D)** St. Jude's rotating disk valve in the open position; **(E)** Hall-Kastor tilting disk valve in the open position; and **(F)** Carpentier-Edwards porcine heterograft valve. For details, see text.

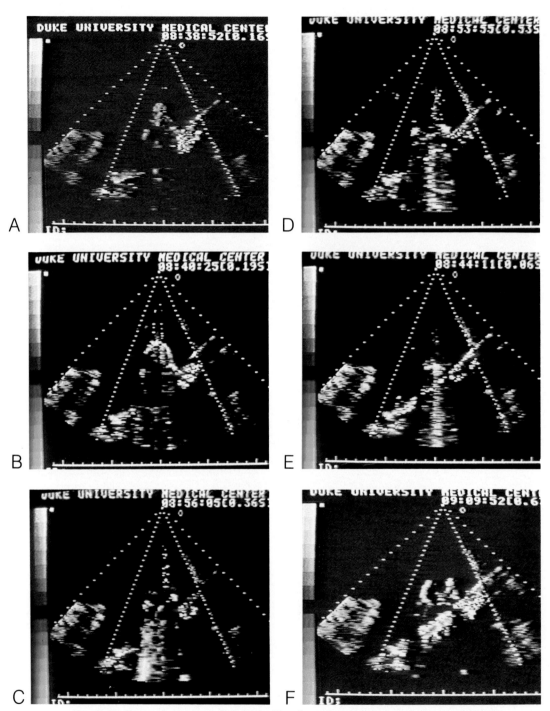

Fig. 9–4. Composite images of flow masking from the various heart valves studied. **(A)** Complete masking of flow behind a Starr-Edwards Silastic ball; **(B)** similar complete masking of flow with a Starr-Edwards stellite ball valve; **(C)** complete masking when the sound passes through the Bjork-Shiley valve; **(D)** only minimum detection of flow behind a St. Jude's valve; **(E)** somewhat more detection of flow behind a Hall-Kastor valve; **(F)** flow is masked only around the sewing ring of a Carpentier-Edwards porcine heterograft. Variance maps were used.

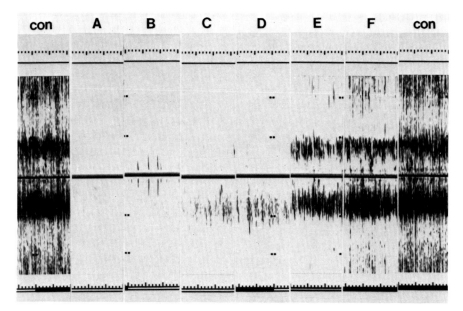

Fig. 9–5. Various spectral recordings of flow behind prosthetic valves using continuous-wave Doppler echocardiography. The control period of flow detection when no valves were in place is shown at either end (con). For details, see text.

sound to penetrate all or portions of the prosthetic valve assembly. The worst penetration was clearly found with the two Starr-Edwards prostheses, each casting a large mask field behind. Very little ultrasound passed the Bjork-Shiley or the St. Jude's valves. Only slightly more could penetrate the Hall-Kastor. Note that this valve's occluding disc has a hole in the very center to allow the disc to interact with the central pivot arm. The Carpentier-Edwards bioprosthesis masked sound only around the valve sewing ring. The central portions of the valve assembly, made up of preserved biologic tissue, allowed the sound to penetrate readily.

The same succession of valves was reexamined using both conventional pulsed and continuous-wave Doppler. Figure 9–5 shows the strong signal obtained from the flow in the tubing during the control (con) periods, which is shown on either end of the figure. Resultant spectral displays from all the valves are shown. Although system gain is held constant, there is a significant reduction in the flow signal resulting from the interposition of the prosthetic valves. Panel A demonstrates no flow detection through a Starr-Edwards valve with Silastic

poppit, Panel B is through a Starr-Edwards valve with stellite poppit, Panel C is through a Bjork-Shiley valve, Panel D is through a St. Jude's valve, Panel E is through a Hall-Kastor valve, and Panel F is through a Carpentier-Edwards porcine valve.

These data have important implications in the clinical setting. These physical properties of prosthetic valves may significantly alter the ability of Doppler systems to detect abnormal flow even when present. Such masks also exist in vitro and evidence for their presence may be found in certain patients. Figure 9–6 demonstrates an apical four-chamber view from a patient with severe residual mitral regurgitation after attempted valvuloplasty using a Carpentier ring. Note the mosaic of regurgitant flow into the left atrium with its lateral borders smoothed by the mask from the prosthetic ring. A lesser degree of mitral regurgitation is seen through a porcine bioprosthesis in Figure 9–7 from the apical four-chamber view. Again, a mask is seen behind the sewing ring on each side and regurgitant flow can only be detected in the center where ultrasound passes through the preserved biologic cusp material.

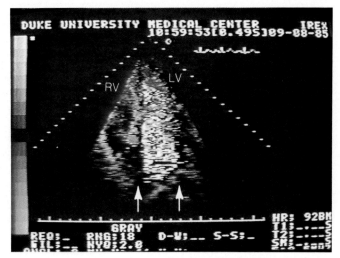

Fig. 9–6. Apical four-chamber view of massive mitral regurgitation in a patient following an attempt at mitral valve annuloplasty using a Carpentier ring. Note the discrete edges on either side of the mitral regurgitant jet indicating the masking effect (arrows). A variance map was used.

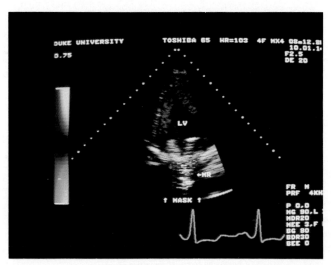

Fig. 9–7. Apical four-chamber view of mitral regurgitation directly through the center portion of a Carpentier-Edwards mitral prosthetic valve. Note the masking effect from the valve ring on either side (arrows). A variance map was used.

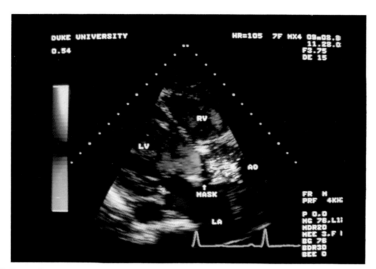

Fig. 9–8. Left parasternal long-axis view of systolic flow through a Carpentier-Edwards porcine heterograft in the aortic position. Note that the suture ring masks the flow. A variance map was used.

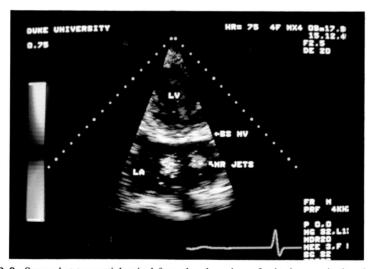

Fig. 9–9. Somewhat tangential apical four-chamber view of mitral regurgitation through a Bjork-Shiley prosthesis. View is obtained from one interspace higher than normal. Flow is detected in the left atrium compatible with mitral regurgitation. At surgery, a thrombus was seen preventing the disc from closing completely. For details, see text. A variance map was used.

Figure 9–8 shows a mask in the left parasternal position from the sewing ring of a porcine bioprosthesis. No flow could be visualized across the aortic diameter masked by the valve ring during any portion of the cardiac cycle. As seen from the previous figures, Carpentier rings and porcine bioprostheses have relatively small areas of masking, generally limited to the area of the valve rings.

Starr-Edwards valves and others have very large areas of masking. For these and the vast majority of other valves comprised of entirely nonbiologic material, the resulting clinical problems due to the large masks are significant. A strong clinical caution must therefore be remembered when encountering patients with prosthetic valves; it may be impossible to detect any flow on the opposite side of a prosthetic valve when the valve is interposed between the interrogating transducer and the area being examined!

The best clinical situation to illustrate this problem is when an operator is examining a patient with a prosthetic mitral valve for mitral regurgitation from the apical views. From this approach, almost the entirety of the left atrium is masked by the prosthesis and the operator could incorrectly conclude that no mitral regurgitation was present. In this case, a very high parasternal view or a subcostal view of the left atrium must be selected for detection of the mitral insufficiency.

The problem is made worse in patients with both aortic and mitral prosthetic valves. The left atrium is inaccessible from the apical views due to the presence of the mitral prosthesis and the aortic prosthesis obscures the left atrium from the parasternal views. In this setting only the subcostal view is available for viewing the left atrium and in our experience this approach is rarely rewarding.

As a result of these observations concerning the difficulty in detecting flow on the far side of a prosthetic valve we always adjust our examination methods to interrogate these valves from all possible views so that the prosthetic valve is not between the transducer and the chamber being examined. This requires considerable operator skill and is true for all Doppler methods. In many instances there is no view available in which the beam can be properly directed. Thus, we strongly suggest that operators of ultrasound equipment do all things possible to properly detect flow. When no flow is detected on the far side of a prosthetic valve it should not be assumed that none is present. We have seen cases of severe valvular regurgitation in which the Doppler examination was rendered artifactually negative due to the masking effect.

There are, however, some exceptions to this rule. In cases where the valve ball or disc is not allowed to seat correctly due to thrombus or vegetation, some sound may be transmitted through the partially open area if it is correctly oriented to the sound beam. Figure 9–9 shows a modified apical four chamber view obtained from one interspace too high and with somewhat inferior angulation in a patient with a Bjork-Shiley prosthetic valve in the mitral position. Two regurgitant jets are seen posterior to the valve ring. There was profound clinical evidence for mitral regurgitation in this patient and at surgery a large thrombus was seen preventing complete closure of the valve disc.

Color Flow Examination of Prosthetic Valves

Color flow imaging provides a means for easy spatial identification of flows through prosthetic valves if the proper transducer orientations and limitations are kept in mind. Figure 9–10 demonstrates an apical four-chamber view of forward diastolic flow through a Starr-Edwards valve in the mitral position. Jets are seen to emerge on both sides of the ball and enter the left ventricle. The jets are symmetric in size and shape when there is orientation of the interrogating beam directly through the center of the flow plane. Remember that diastolic flow through a Starr-Edwards valve is conical in three dimensions. Too low or too high angulation will cause the scan plane to intercept the flow cone on its edge resulting in only one jet being visualized.

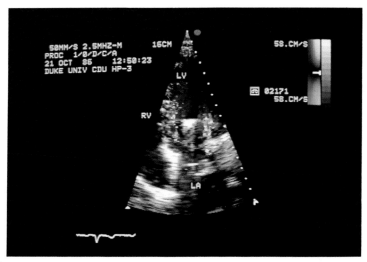

Fig. 9–10. Apical four-chamber view of normal diastolic flow through a Starr-Edwards mitral posthesis. Note that the flow on either side of the ball is symmetric. A variance map was used; spatial filters are off.

When the prosthetic valve has not been between the transducer and the chamber of interest, abnormal flows may be detected. Figure 9–11 demonstrates abnormal diastolic flow compatible with periprosthetic leaks from a Starr-Edwards valve in the aortic position. The image is in the parasternal long axis.

Color flow imaging provides a means to easily differentiate the turbulent forward flow through a mitral prosthesis from that of aortic regurgitation. Figure 9–12 is a parasternal long-axis view in diastole showing the aortic regurgitation in a patient with a mitral valve prosthesis originating at the level of the aortic valve. Note that the Starr-Edwards valve in the mitral position completely masks flow behind it.

Figure 9–13 is an image of normal diastolic flow through a Bjork-Shiley prosthetic valve as imaged from the apical four-chamber view. Note carefully that forward flow can be seen through both the major and minor orifices of the valve when the prosthesis is functioning normally. As seen in this example, the area of flow through the larger orifice is roughly two or more times larger than the area of flow

through the minor orifice. Since the Bjork-Shiley valve is a tilting disc, forward flow should always be imaged through both. When it is not, thrombus or other material may be occluding one or the other orifice. Note that in Figure 9–3 this valve has a lesser orifice and a greater orifice so that normal forward flow will never be symmetric.

Forward flow through a bioprosthesis usually fills the entirety of the valve orifice under normal conditions. Figure 9–14 shows a typical left parasternal long axis image of a normally functioning Carpentier-Edwards bioprosthesis in the mitral position during diastole. A central core of aliasing with reversed color is frequently seen in this situation, probably as a result of the mildly constricted orifice due to the presence of the artificial valve ring. There have been no studies into the variable appearances of abnormal diastolic jets through porcine valves. Figure 9–15 demonstrates another appearance of a normal functioning bioprosthesis from the apical four-chamber view. There is a diffuse mosaic and a readily noted area of color on the atrial side of the prosthesis.

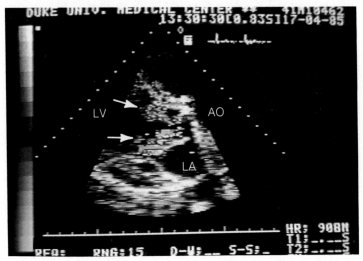

Fig. 9–11. Parasternal long-axis view showing the aortic regurgitation on either side of a Starr-Edwards valve in the aortic position in diastole. Multiple periprosthetic leaks were noted all around the suture ring (arrows). A variance map was used.

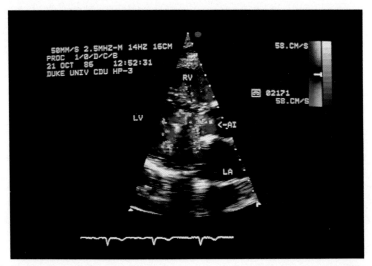

Fig. 9–12. Parasternal long-axis view showing aortic regurgitation from a patient with a Starr-Edwards valve in the mitral position. Note the masking of flow by the prosthesis. A variance map was used; spatial filters are off.

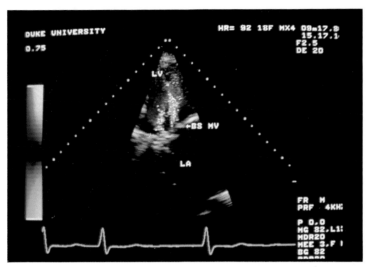

Fig. 9–13. Apical four-chamber view of normal diastolic flow of a Bjork-Shiley mitral prosthesis. Note that these two jets are not symmetric. The smaller comes from the lesser orifice while the larger of the jets emerge through the greater orifice. A variance map was used.

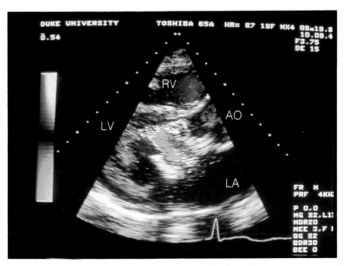

Fig. 9–14. Parasternal long-axis view showing normal diastolic flow through a Carpentier-Edwards mitral valve prosthesis. Normally, flow fills the orifice of the prosthesis. A variance map was used.

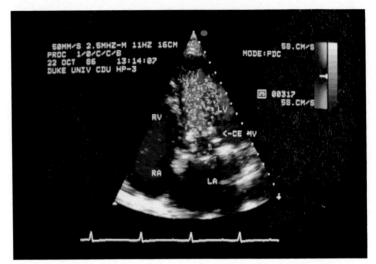

Fig. 9–15. Apical four-chamber view of a normally functioning Carpentier-Edwards mitral bioprosthesis. There is a diffuse mosaic throughout the left ventricle in diastole. Note the area of coloration on the atrial side of the valve. A variance map was used; spatial filters are off.

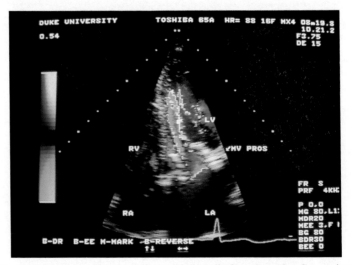

Fig. 9–16. Apical two-chamber view of normal diastolic flow through a Carpentier-Edwards mitral valve prosthesis. A variance map was used.

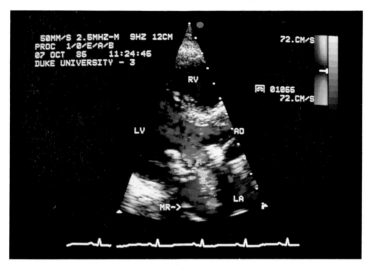

Fig. 9–17. Parasternal long-axis view of mitral regurgitation through the center of a porcine mitral prosthesis. Note the masking of the left atrium behind the anterior strut of the prosthesis. A variance map was used; spatial filters are on.

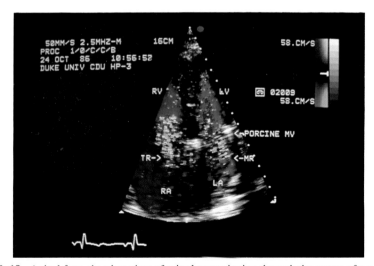

Fig. 9–18. Apical four-chamber view of mitral regurgitation through the center of a porcine mitral prosthesis. A variance map was used; spatial filters are off.

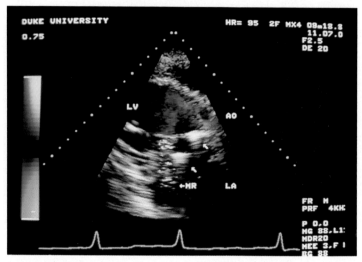

Fig. 9–19. Left parasternal long-axis view in systole showing abnormal flow posterior to the valve ring into the left atrium. This is compatible with a periprosthetic leak. The arrows indicate the location of the prosthetic valve ring. A variance map was used.

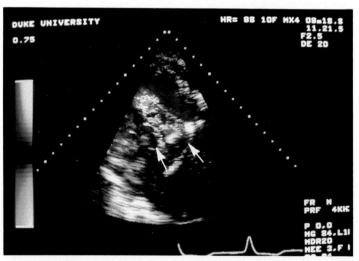

Fig. 9–20. Parasternal long-axis diastolic flow image of the same individual seen in the previous figure. Note that forward flow is imaged through the orifice of the prosthetic valve as well as through the posterior periprosthetic leak (arrows). A variance map was used.

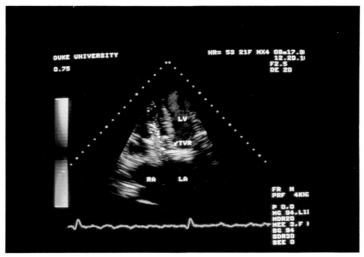

Fig. 9–21. Apical four-chamber view of normal diastolic flow through a tricuspid Carpentier-Edwards porcine heterograft. The flow is quite similar in appearance to that through a similar valve in the mitral position. A variance map was used.

Figure 9–16 demonstrates an apical two-chamber view of the same mitral porcine prosthesis seen in the previous figure. From the apex, the forward flow is even more striking when the complete jet is visualized nearly to the apex of the left ventricle.

Since little masking is seen from porcine valves, color flow is frequently able to detect valvular insufficiency in this setting. Figure 9–17 demonstrates a parasternal long axis view of prosthetic mitral regurgitation through the center of a Carpentier-Edwards bioprosthesis. Note the masking behind the anterior strut. Figure 9–18 demonstrates prosthetic mitral regurgitation from the apical four-chamber approach

in another patient with a porcine heterograft prosthesis.

Occasionally a perivalvular leak may be visualized as is seen in the patient in Figure 9–19. A small mitral regurgitant jet is seen posterior to the ring of a porcine prosthesis (arrows) in systole. In diastole (Fig. 9–20), forward flow can be seen through the prosthetic valve orifice as well as the perivalvular area posteriorly.

Normal forward flow through a porcine prosthesis in the tricuspid position resembles that in the mitral position. Figure 9–21 shows a central core of aliasing through a Carpentier-Edwards prosthesis as visualized in the apical four-chamber position.

10

Color Flow Imaging of Common Congenital Disorders

It is well known that two-dimensional echocardiography has had a major impact on the care of patients with congenital heart disorders. It is unparalleled in its ability to detect anatomic disorders by the spatial display of anatomic information. Conventional Doppler methods have made an additional contribution and methods are available to detect the presence of intracardiac shunting as well as to quantitate such things as the relative ratios of pulmonary to systemic blood flows. Readers are directed to textbooks of two-dimensional echocardiography and conventional Doppler methods for discussions of these important applications.

Color flow Doppler also has a very useful role in the assessment of congenital abnormalities. By superimposing flow data on the two-dimensional echocardiogram, abnormal flows are easily recognized in many disorders. When examining small infants, there is frequently little time to perform a complete conventional pulsed Doppler examination. When complex anatomy is encountered, use of blind conventional continuous-wave Doppler is frequently complicated by the absence of usual flow landmarks that assure the user of beam location.

Our intent in this chapter is to briefly present several examples of the more common congenital abnormalities. The color flow imaging approach speeds the Doppler examination in patients with congenital heart disease and in some cases obviates the use of conventional methods. As explained in detail in Chapter 3, however, serious frame rate limitations are imposed upon color flow images that sometimes may prevent adequate assessment of flows in very tiny infants with rapid heart rates.

Atrial Septal Defect

In infants and small children, atrial septal defects are frequently directly visualized using two-dimensional echocardiography. In adults, the situation is somewhat different as difficulties with image quality and other factors limit detection of the actual defect. Figure 10–1 demonstrates flow from a pulmonary vein directly across an atrial septal defect from the subcostal view in a 32-year-old woman in whom there was little indication of the presence of such a defect on the two-dimensional image alone.

In our experience, it is quite difficult for beginners in the use of conventional methods to understand the spectral displays resulting from

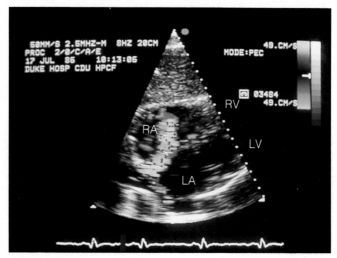

Fig. 10–1. Subcostal view of interatrial shunting. Flow is seen to emerge from a pulmonary vein and cross the interatrial septum into the right atrium. An enhanced map was used; spatial filters are on.

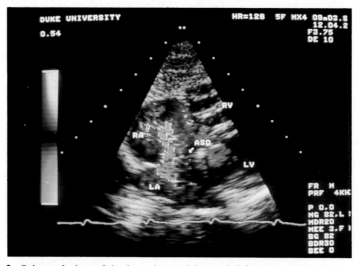

Fig. 10–2. Subcostal view of the large interatrial septal defect in a child. The central core of aliasing is seen through the atrial septal defect. A turbulence map was used.

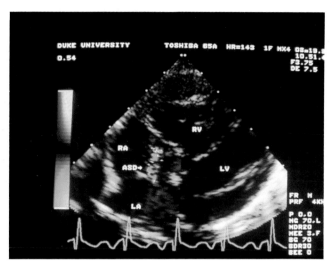

Fig. 10–3. Small atrial septal defect in a young child. Note that the flow never fills the suspected area of the anatomic defect. A turbulence map was used.

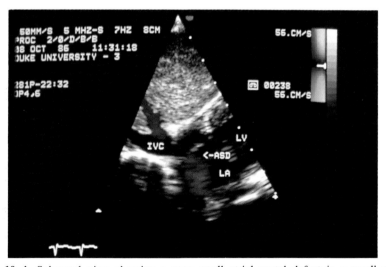

Fig. 10–4. Subcostal view showing a very small atrial septal defect in a small child. There is negligible flow detected across the interatrial septum. A turbulence map was used; spatial filters are off.

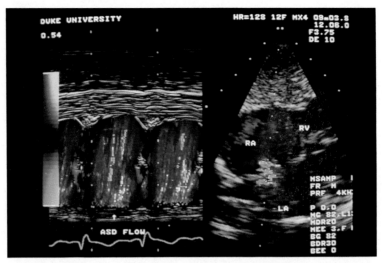

Fig. 10–5. On the right is a subcostal view of an atrial septal defect with its flow from left atrium to right atrium. The color M-mode frequently helps to time flow events. A turbulence map was used.

abnormal interatrial flows. Vena caval and coronary sinus inflows frequently make interpretation of subtle changes in the conventional spectral Doppler velocity display of right atrial inflow difficult. This problem is further complicated when the examiner encounters congenital heart disorders in only rare instances.

Color flow imaging helps tremendously in identifying patients with interatrial shunting. The subcostal views are clearly the best for this purpose as the interatrial septum is oriented perpendicular to the sound beam and readily visualized while any abnormal flow through the septum is parallel to the beam and toward the transducer.

Figure 10–2 shows a large left-to-right flow from the left atrium to the right atrium through a large atrial septal defect in a child. In fact, the anatomic limits of the defect may be more clearly defined by the image of the flow in relationship to the anatomic target information.

Figure 10–3 demonstrates a smaller atrial septal defect flow orifice, again in a small child. Aliasing is readily seen within the abnormal jet in the right atrium because a 3.75-MHz transducer was used. Note that the defect appears larger on the anatomic portion of the image than on the flow image. The overall color gains were optimally set by the operator and flow was never seen to fill the entire defect as displayed on the two-dimensional image alone. Even a marked increase in color gain could not increase the flow area through the suspected orifice. These discrepancies occasionally occur and are probably due to the fact that the interatrial septum is not always a strong reflector of ultrasound. An even smaller amount of flow is seen across the interatrial septum in the infant shown in Figure 10–4. Here, trivial interatrial shunting is seen.

These abnormal flow patterns appear to be very specific for interatrial communications. To date, however, there have been no large, blinded studies attesting to either the specificity or the sensitivity of this approach. Until the advent of color flow imaging in our laboratory we placed the greatest confidence in the microcavitation technique for the detection of interatrial shunts and had little confidence in conventional approaches. Now color flow imaging is our first choice for diagnosing this disorder. Only rarely do we now resort to injections of microcavita-

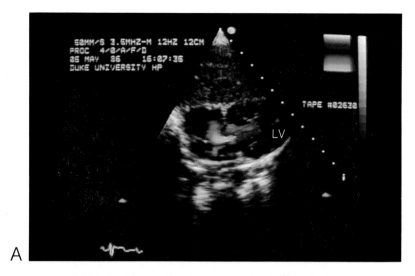

A

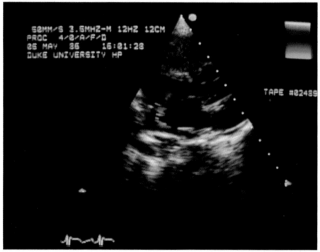

B

Fig. 10–6. (A) Subcostal view of flow from the right atrium across an interatrial septal defect into the left atrium and orifice of an atrial ventricular valve. **(B)** Left-to-right atrial flow in the same individual. These images were obtained from a 1-year-old child with a hypoplastic right heart. Enhanced maps were used; spatial filters are on.

tions. In most of these cases the interatrial shunting is of minor degree.

Simultaneous color M-mode displays may also be used for more precise timing of events. Such a display is shown in Figure 10–5 where turbulent flow toward the transducer (left-to-right) is seen throughout systole.

It is also possible to simply use color flow imaging to confirm the presence of obligatory interatrial shunting in more complex lesions. Figure 10–6 shows bidirectional shunting in an infant with an absent right atrioventricular connection and a hypoplastic right heart from the subcostal approach. Figure 10–6A shows the right-to-left component while Figure 10–6B shows the left-to-right component.

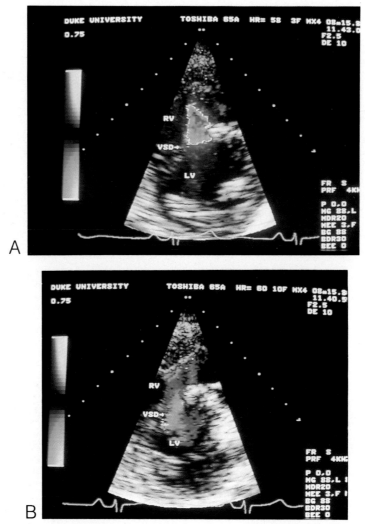

Fig. 10–7. (A) Left parasternal short-axis view of the left ventricle; the left-to-right component of flow is shown through a very large ventricular septal defect. **(B)** Right-to-left component of flow is visualized. A turbulence map was used.

Ventricular Septal Defect

Most clinically significant ventricular septal defects in infants are readily imaged with two-dimensional echocardiography. In adults, it is rare to find a totally unsuspected ventricular septal defect that is large. Figure 10–7 shows a very large ventricular septal defect in a 30-year-old woman with Eisenmenger physiology (marked elevation of pulmonary pressures in excess of systemic) from the left parasternal short-axis view of the left ventricle. Systolic flow from left to right is seen as a bright burst of red with a central core of aliasing (Fig.10–7A). The diastolic image from the same patient shows the right-to-left component in blue (Fig. 10–7B).

Of course, most such defects are small and

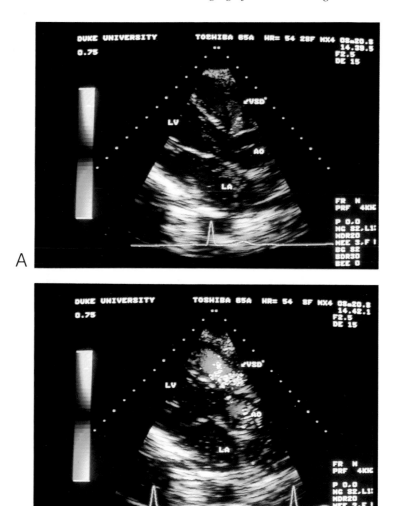

Fig. 10–8. (A) Parasternal long-axis view in diastole of a left-to-right shunt from a ventricular septal defect. Note that the mean velocity estimates are low as seen by the dull hues of color. (B) In systole the gradient between ventricles is increased and there is a bright mosaic of turbulent flow. A variance map was used.

difficult to image directly. Despite the ready detection of larger defects in children, these smaller defects are nearly impossible to image using two-dimensional echocardiography in adults. Conventional pulsed Doppler is very reliable for detection of these abnormal flows but the process is long and arduous as it involves complex mapping of all portions of the interventricular septum.

With color flow imaging, however, these defects are easily seen. Figure 10–8 shows typical serial frames from a patient with a small ventricular septal defect in the subaortic area. During diastole there is a small jet from left to right imaged in hues of red (Fig. 10–8A). During systole the jet becomes markedly turbulent as mean velocity estimates are high and a bright mosaic of the shunt flow is seen (Fig. 10–8B).

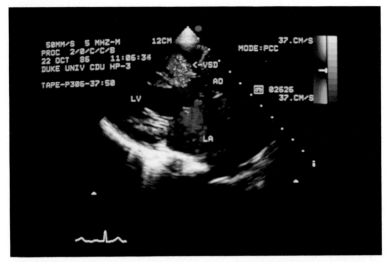

Fig. 10–9. Left parasternal long-axis view of a 4-year-old child with a small ventricular septal defect. Note the very bright mosaic of aliasing resulting because of a large gradient between the ventricles. A variance map was used; spatial filters are off.

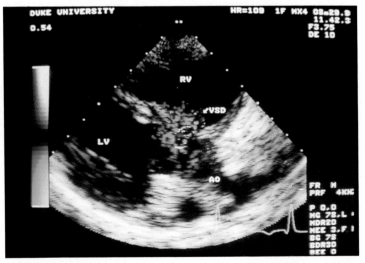

Fig. 10–10. Parasternal long-axis view of interventricular shunting from a 5-year-old child with a large ventricle septal defect. Note that the mosaic is less prominent in this instance. A variance map was used.

Figure 10–9 demonstrates a similar systolic phenomenon in a 4-year-old child with a ventricular septal defect and a congenital cleft of the mitral valve with severe mitral regurgitation. A 3 m/sec systolic aortic jet was detected by continuous-wave Doppler across the ventricular septal defect. Note the prominent mosaic of the abnormal flow resulting from the ventricular septal defect. When pressure differences between the ventricles are marked and

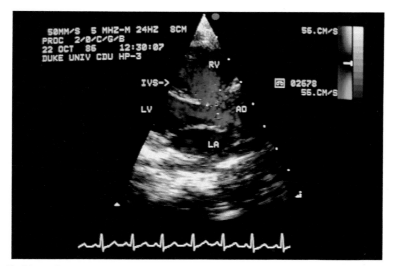

Fig. 10–11. Left parasternal long-axis view of flow emerging from both the right and left ventricle and entering an overriding aorta in a patient with tetralogy of Fallot. Since severe pulmonic stenosis was present, the pressures between the two ventricles were approximately the same. For details, see text. A variance map was used; spatial filters are off.

the defect is small, very high mean velocity estimates result, severe aliasing occurs, and such prominent mosaic patterns result. Compare the appearance of this abnormal flow with that of the adult patient with nearly equal pressures in the right and left ventricles in Figure 10–7 where there is less turbulence and a less prominent mosaic.

When the size of the ventricular septal defect is large and the pressure differences between the ventricles are less marked, the mean estimates of flow velocity calculated by the color flow imaging devices are low. Figure 10–10 shows a less prominent mosaic with less aliasing than in the last patient.

In tetralogy of Fallot, the aorta overrides the interventricular septum and there is usually a large ventricular septal defect. In addition, pulmonary stenosis is present and is occasionally severe. Figure 10–11 demonstrates a parasternal long-axis systolic image with left ventricular blood flow merging with right ventricular blood flow that crosses the large septal defect; both flows then enter the overriding aorta. This image was obtained in a 5-month-old boy with severe pulmonary stenosis and equal pressures

within the ventricles. Little aliasing is seen because of the lack of a pressure difference.

Right-to-left components of shunting may also be detected. Figure 10–12 shows such systolic direction of flow in a premature infant with transposition of the great vessels where the shunt is directed across the ventricular septal defect into the proximal pulmonary artery.

The flow study image in Figure 10–13 was obtained from a 26-year-old woman who underwent repair of a pseudotruncus arteriosus several years earlier. In that repair a graft conduit was placed from the right ventricle to the pulmonary arteries and a ventricular septal defect was closed. She was clinically suspected of having a small residual ventricular septal defect. Conventional pulsed Doppler examination detected a left-to-right shunt and the point of origin seemed very high on the ventricular septum. The color flow examination readily showed the defect to be originating from the very large aortic root and directed into the right ventricle.

As with so many disorders, the color flow examination may be used to direct a continuous-wave Doppler examination. Figure 10–14 shows a spectral recording resulting from a con-

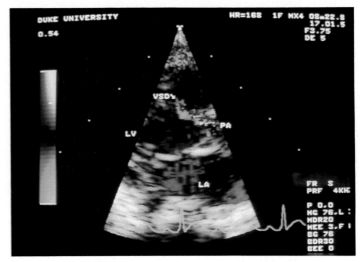

Fig. 10–12. Parasternal long-axis view from a premature infant with transposition of the great vessels. Flow is seen to cross from the anterior right ventricle through a ventricular septal defect into the pulmonary artery. A variance map was used.

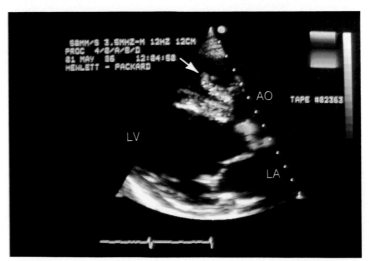

Fig. 10–13. Parasternal long-axis view showing shunting from the aorta to the right ventricle (arrow) in a patient with pseudotruncus arteriosus. An enhanced map was used; spatial filters are on.

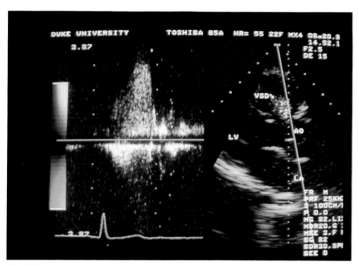

Fig. 10–14. Color flow imaging may be used to guide a continuous-wave Doppler beam. At the right is a parasternal long-axis image of flow through a ventricular septal defect. A continuous-wave beam (dotted line) depicts the direction of the beam. At the left is the spectral recording. A variance map was used.

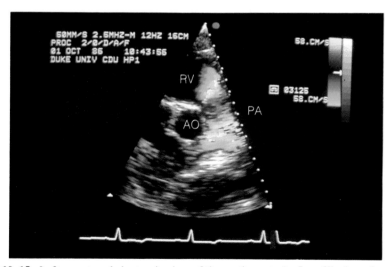

Fig. 10–15. Left parasternal short-axis view of the aortic root. As flow fills the pulmonary artery in peak systole a bright mosaic of color is seen in normal individuals. An enhanced map was used; spatial filters are on.

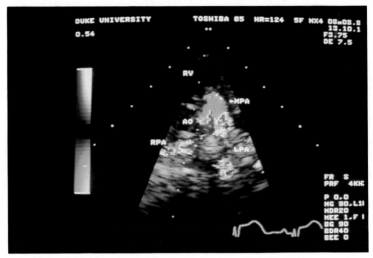

Fig. 10–16. Parasternal short-axis view of the aortic root. In disorders such as ductus arteriosus, turbulent flow is seen within the pulmonary arteries as a result of shunting. A turbulence map was used.

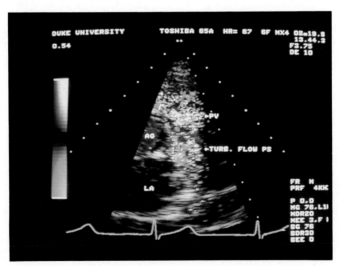

Fig. 10–17. Turbulence within the pulmonary artery is also seen with disorders such as pulmonic stenosis. A parasternal short-axis view of the aortic root and proximal pulmonary artery is seen. Note the turbulent flow. A variance map was used.

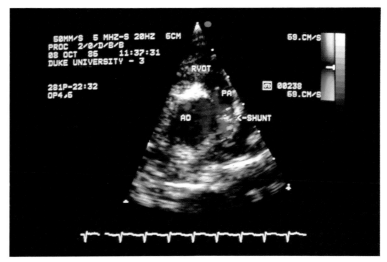

Fig. 10–18. Parasternal short-axis view of the aortic root showing turbulence in the proximal pulmonary artery resulting from large flow through a Blalock-Taussig shunt. For details, see text. A variance map was used; spatial filters are off.

Other Congenital Anomalies

tinuous-wave beam directed through the ventricular septal defect (dotted line).

Among the many other congenital anomalies in which color flow is useful is in the detection of ductus arteriosus. Normal flow through the pulmonary valve and proximal pulmonary artery is usually laminar. At peak systole, a wide area of central aliasing occurs as shown in Figure 10–15. Rarely is turbulence encountered in this area.

In ductus arteriosus there is a connection between the aorta and the pulmonary artery that is frequently associated with severe shunting into the pulmonary circuit. When this occurs, turbulence and higher mean velocity estimates are detected by the flow imaging device and much of the proximal pulmonary artery is filled with a mosaic of bright colors (Fig. 10–16).

Unfortunately, other lesions such as pulmonic stenosis also result in such a prominent pattern in the proximal pulmonary artery. Figure 10–17 demonstrates the typical pattern resulting from such stenosis in the parasternal short-axis view of the aortic root. Conventional Doppler methods are almost always necessary to precisely differentiate these two lesions.

Occasionally, flows from various surgical shunts can be visualized and confirmed. The parasternal short-axis view at the level of the aortic root shown in Figure 10–18 shows turbulence within the pulmonary artery from a Blalock-Taussig shunt in an infant with complex congenital heart disease. The proper diagnosis of a disorder leading to pulmonary artery turbulence depends upon knowledge of prior surgical procedures and proper use of conventional Doppler methods.

11

Color Flow Imaging of Myxomas, Masses, and Missiles

Color flow imaging provides additional information concerning patients with mass lesions of the heart valves and heart chambers. In our limited experience with patients with these disorders, it appears that the spatial representation of flow information is the key to detecting unsuspected complications. Ease of conducting a color flow examination helps the operator in deriving useful information. Because some of these lesions are so rare, useful information can only be presented in an anecdotal format. This chapter is prepared as a series of case presentations, each discussing the additional information delivered by the color flow approach.

Cardiac Tumors and Clots

Figure 11–1 shows chest radiographs from a 52-year-old woman who was admitted to our institution with a 1-day history of shortness of breath. The left atrium appears enlarged. Previously in very good health, she found she could not complete her usual round of 18 holes of golf. On physical examination, she had murmurs suspicious for mitral stenosis and insufficiency.

Color flow examination revealed an extraor-dinarily large left atrial mass typical of a myxoma. Flow could be seen to move around the tumor mass and enter the mitral valve orifice in the parasternal long axis view (Fig. 11–2). Left with these data alone, it appeared obvious that surgical removal of the mass lesion was indicated.

On further examination in the left parasternal short-axis view of the left atrium, the point of attachment of the tumor mass could be seen as broad based and without the typical tumor stalk seen in patients with left atrial myxoma. A part of the tumor could also be seen extruding through the ostium secundum of the interatrial septum into the right atrial cavity. A small jet of flow was readily detected originating near the ostium secundum and directed toward the tricuspid valve orifice (Fig. 11–3).

The broad tumor attachment site and the fact that it extended through the interatrial septum helped to plan the surgical approach. It was quite likely that both atria would have to be opened with extensive resection of the interatrial septum in order for the tumor to be delivered easily.

Based on these data and without cardiac catheterization, the patient underwent tumor removal where the right atrium was first incised.

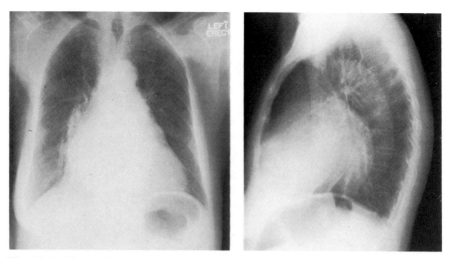

Fig. 11–1. Chest radiographs of a patient with the relatively sudden onset of shortness of breath. The left atrium is enlarged.

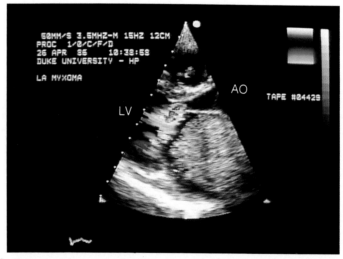

Fig. 11–2. Parasternal long-axis view showing a massive left atrial tumor. In other views, the point of attachment of the tumor was broad based. An enhanced map was used; spatial filters are on.

The mass was confirmed to be present through the ostium secundum; gentle pressure could not remove the mass from the orifice. A left atrial incision revealed the bulk of the tumor as seen in Figure 11–4A. In this figure, the patient's head is toward the top and feet are toward the bottom. The left atrium has been pulled posteriorly around to the left of the image. Various tubes and other instruments are present that are required for cardiopulmonary bypass. Following extensive removal of the interatrial septum the mass was finally delivered along with its broad point of attachment (Fig. 11–4B). Further details of this patient's operative removal and repair as guided by the color flow imaging system are presented in Chapter 12.

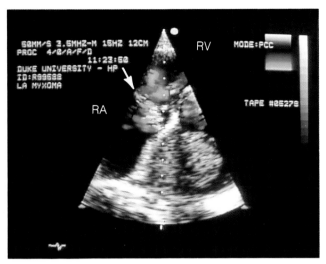

Fig. 11–3. Modified apical four-chamber view of the previous patient. A jet could be seen emerging from the base of the ostium secundum (arrow). In other views, a part of the tumor mass was seen to extrude through the fossa ovalis. An enhanced map was used; spatial filters are on.

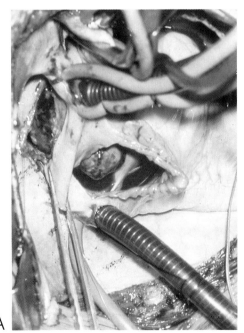
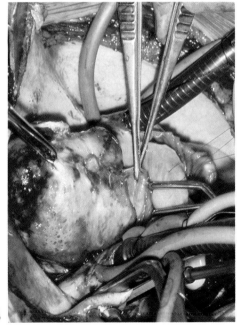

A   B

Fig. 11–4. Surgical views of the removal of the tumor mass. The patient's head is toward the top and feet are toward the bottom. **(A)** The left atrium has been pulled posterior and appears at the left. The right atrium has been opened, and a portion of the tumor extruding through the fossa ovalis is seen. **(B)** Final delivery of the tumor mass. Note the broad based attachments to the interatrial septum.

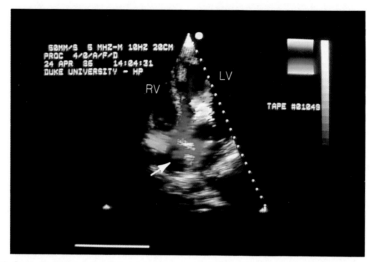

Fig. 11–5. Apical four-chamber view from a patient with suspicious evidence of a right atrial mass. Note the absence of flow within the right atrium (arrow). For details, see text. An enhanced map was used; spatial filters were on.

Fig. 11–6. (A) Surgical photographs of the removal of the right atrial mass. **(B)** Dimension of the excised mass. For details, see text.

Other Atrial Masses

There are, of course, other intracavitary masses that may imitate atrial tumors. Occasionally, color flow systems may reveal important information by the absence of flow in a given area, an effect resembling negative contrast on an angiogram.

Figure 11–5 shows a color flow image from the apical four chamber view in a 69-year-old woman who was admitted with progressive dyspnea. Her conventional two-dimensional echocardiographic study was of very poor quality. Both left and right ventricles appeared to be of normal size and have normal movement. There was a suspicion of a right atrial mass lesion but poor image quality precluded certain diagnosis, even following saline contrast study. Color flow study, however, showed an area adjacent to the free wall of the right atrium where flow could not be detected. After the same effect was observed in multiple views, the strong suspicion of an intracavitary mass lesion in the right atrium was raised. This was enough evidence to proceed with right atrial cineangiography where the presence of the mass lesion was confirmed.

The patient underwent surgical removal of the mass, and the intraoperative photos are shown in Figure 11–6. Again, the patient's head is toward the top and feet are toward the bottom of the illustration. Figure 11–6A reveals the mass lesion within the right atrium just after atriotomy, and Figure 11–6B demonstrates the excised mass, which was later determined on microscopic section to be a large blood clot. Further details of the use of transesophageal color flow in this patient are presented in Chapter 12.

The absence of flow detection in an area where flow is usually present may raise the suspicion for the presence of a space-occupying mass lesion, but there is too little experience with this application to place certainty on the diagnostic findings. This case does, however, illustrate the rare instance where such a finding may direct further patient evaluation and therapy.

Missiles

Missile wounds of the heart are exceedingly rare. We have encountered a variety of such wounds over the years resulting from bullets, shot, and other similar objects. Our experience indicates that there is no certainty of the path of the missile once it enters the chest and we have been surprised to find that pericardial effusions result in only 50 percent of penetrating heart injuries and there is a surprisingly high incidence of unsuspected intracardiac shunting that may result from such trauma.

Figure 11–7 shows the chest of a 19-year-old man admitted to our emergency room from a housing construction site after experiencing the sudden onset of chest pain. A bright object is seen in the center of the lower thorax that was circular and moving in synchrony with the heart cycle. His chest radiograph is shown in Figure 11–8, where a large nail is readily observed. On further questioning, he indicated that he worked with a pneumatic nail gun that fires nails at extreme velocity and that he avoids the use of a traditional hammer. The gun accidentally discharged while the worker cavorted with friends during a lunch break.

The quality of the initial two-dimensional echo and conventional Doppler examination was compromised by the patient's respiratory distress and chest pain. The nail could be seen to enter the apical portion of the free wall of the right ventricle and traverse the right ventricular cavity with the tip just resting adjacent to the interventricular septum. Emergency thoracotomy was performed because of hemodynamic compromise, and the nail was removed under direct visualization. Green dyes performed at the time of surgery failed to reveal intracardiac shunting.

Follow-up color flow evaluation showed a small ventricular septal defect near the insertion of the tricuspid valve apparatus that was readily detected (Fig. 11–9). Serial evaluation over several months showed the development of an aneurysmal sac and ultimate closure of the traumatic defect.

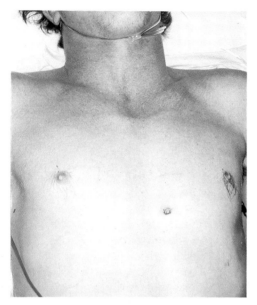

Fig. 11–7. Photograph of the chest of an individual admitted with the sudden onset of chest pain. Note the bright object at the lower left poriton of the sternum.

Masses

The most common intracardiac masses are those resulting from vegetative endocarditis. Several patients with this disorder have been persented in earlier chapters. Of note, however, is the fact that the spatial representation of abnormal flow seen by color flow imaging frequently aids the surgeon in planning the approach to surgical replacement or repair.

Figure 11–10 demonstrates paired parasternal long axis views from a young woman with bacterial endocarditis and acute, severe mitral insufficiency. Figure 11–10A shows one jet of mitral regurgitation originating at the mitral orifice while Figure 11–10B demonstrates another jet originating at the mid portion of the anterior mitral valve leaflet. Detected vegetative masses were very small. On the basis of these findings primary leaflet repair, rather than replacement, was planned.

At surgery a small hole was found in the anterior mitral valve leaflet and multiple small

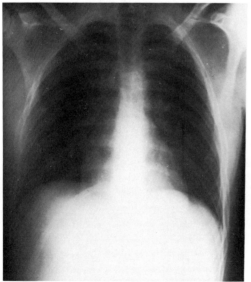
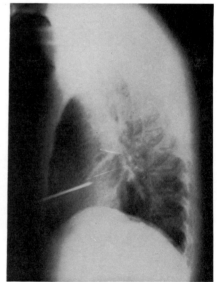

Fig. 11–8. Chest radiographs of the patient in Figure 11–7. A nail is seen entering the cardiac silhouette.

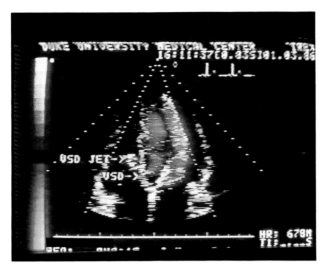

Fig. 11–9. Parasternal long-axis view showing a ventricular septal defect with flow entering the right ventricle. The flow emerges from the upper portions of the interventricular septum near the insertion of the tricuspid valve. For details, see text. A variance map was used.

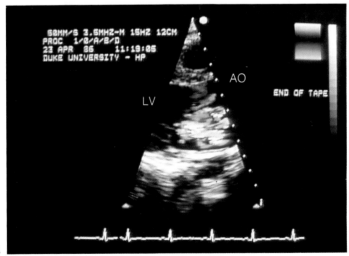

A

Fig. 11–10. Parasternal long-axis view from a patient with bacterial endocarditis. (**A**) A large mitral regurgitant jet can be seen within the left atrium entering from the mitral orifice. (*Figure continues.*)

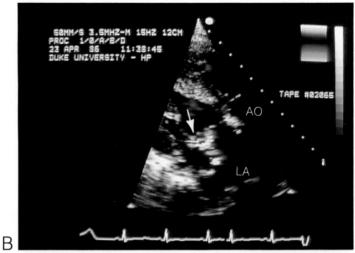

B

Fig. 11–10 (*Continued*). Slight angulation where a second regurgitant jet enters the left atrium through the mid portion of the anterior mitral valve leaflet (arrow). Enhanced maps were used; spatial filters were on.

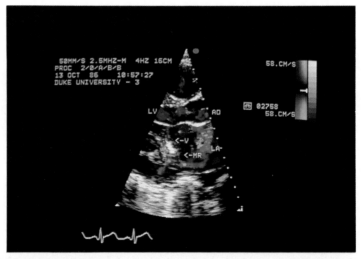

Fig. 11–11. Parasternal long-axis view from another patient with vegetative endocarditis. A large vegetative mass can be seen within the left atrium. The flow emerges from the mitral valve orifice and proceeds posteriorly to the mass lesion. A variance map was used; spatial filters were off.

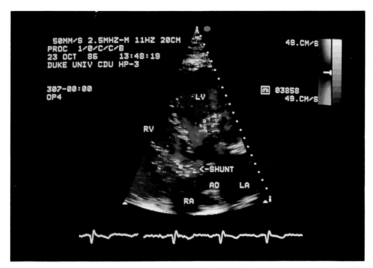

Fig. 11–12. Apical four-chamber view from patient with vegetative endocarditis of the septal leaflet of the tricuspid valve. A fistulous tract had developed between the right atrium and aorta resulting in a continuous mosaic. A turbulence map was used; spatial filters are off.

vegetations were found on the tips of both leaflets. The vegetations were debrided, and the involved area of the anterior mitral leaflet was resected and replaced with a transplanted portion of the posterior leaflet. The posterior leaflet was then repaired. On serial follow-up color flow study the patient has trivial residual mitral regurgitation.

Thus, the spatial display of flow is what makes the Doppler information readily usable in these patients. Figure 11–11 reveals a parasternal long axis view of a 20-year-old heroin addict with a large vegetative mass resulting from *Streptococcus viridans*. The mitral regurgitant jet originates at the mitral orifice and is directed posterior to the mass lesion. In this setting it appeared unlikely that repair of the mitral valve would be fruitful. Operative intervention was performed on the basis of the echo

and color flow data alone and the tips of the mitral leaflets were found to be severely eroded by the infectious process and beyond primary repair. A prosthetic mitral valve was inserted.

Too frequently, the masses of vegetative endocarditis distract the operator's attention during the echocardiographic examination. One should always think of the potential complication resulting from the disorder and color flow allows rapid investigation for abnormal flows. Figure 11–12 shows an apical four-chamber view from a patient with endocarditis involving the septal leaflet of the tricuspid valve. With slight superior angulation a continuously present mosaic of abnormal flow was seen emerging from the aortic root into the right atrium. In this patient a fistulous tract had developed as a consequence of the infectious process. The patient is now awaiting a repair.

12

Transesophageal Color Flow Imaging

Norbert P. de Bruijn, M.D.
Fiona M. Clements, M.D.

Color flow Doppler methods can also be used from the transesophageal approach. Imaging from the esophagus overcomes difficulties in obtaining good image quality from the chest wall that are commonly encountered in obese patients and those with emphysema. Perhaps the most important use for transesophageal imaging is during open heart surgery. It allows direct observation of the movement of the heart walls and valves prior to, and just after, surgical procedures. With the advent of color flow capabilities, this approach now provides a means for evaluating certain conditions, guiding the surgical approach and evaluating the results during the operative procedure.

The Transesophageal Approach

Transesophageal images are obtained using a transducer mounted on the end of an endoscope with the fiber optic material removed and replaced with the various wires to the transducer head. Figure 12–1 illustrates a 64-element, 5-mHz transducer which measures 9 × 12 mm, and is incorporated onto the end of a flexible gastroscope from which the fiberoptics have been removed. The transducer tip is manipula-

ble to allow the operator to properly orient the scan plane to the heart. Without the chest wall intervening between transducer and heart, the two-dimensional images are generally of high quality. This allows the use of higher-frequency transducers and results in much better definition of cardiac structures.

The left atrium and left ventricle lying posteriorly in the thorax are most advantageously imaged from an esophageal approach as shown in the schematic diagram in Figure 12–2. With color flow or conventional Doppler, a further advantage of the esophageal transducer becomes apparent. When the esophageal transducer is positioned behind the left atrium and directed toward the cardiac apex, the ultrasound beam is aligned in parallel with the majority of normal intracardiac blood flow through the mitral valve (Fig. 12–3). In particular, this provides excellent conditions for the detection of mitral regurgitation and high-velocity jets of flow through a stenotic mitral valve.

Those who are familiar only with the transthoracic images require some orientation to transesophageal images. Figure 12–4 demonstrates a color flow image from the four chamber approach in diastole. The transducer is adjacent to the left atrium, which therefore appears up-

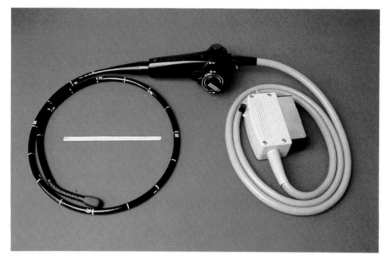

Fig. 12–1. Hewlett-Packard 64-element, 5-MHz transesophageal probe (prototype). The external diameter of the shaft is 9 mm. The external controls for flexion–extension and sideways movement can be seen.

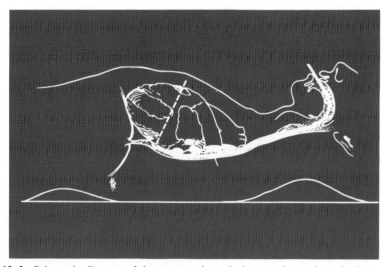

Fig. 12–2. Schematic diagram of the transesophageal ultrasound transducer in the esophagus. The transducer is positioned behind the left ventricle in order to obtain a short-axis image.

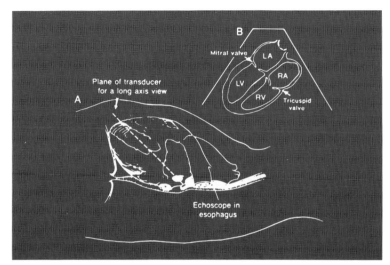

Fig. 12–3. Transesophageal ultrasound transducer positioned behind the left atrium. The tip is "overextended" so that the beam is directed anteroinferiorly, producing a four-chamber view.

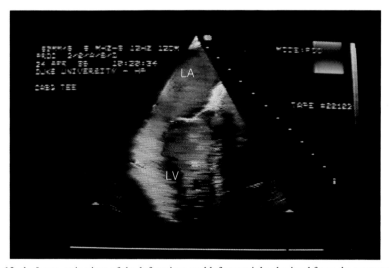

Fig. 12–4. Long-axis view of the left atrium and left ventricle obtained from the transesophageal approach in diastole. Note the flow through the mitral valve orifice. An enhanced map was used; spatial filters are on. This image was obtained from videotape and therefore is somewhat different in quality from images in other chapters.

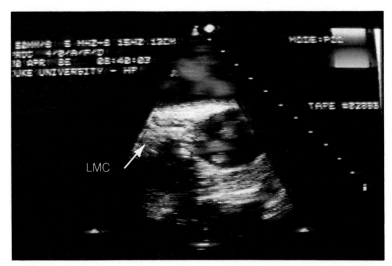

Fig. 12–5. Short-axis view of the aortic root showing flow in the proximal left coronary artery in a normal volunteer. An enhanced map was used; spatial filters are on. This image was obtained from videotape and therefore is somewhat different in quality from images in other chapters.

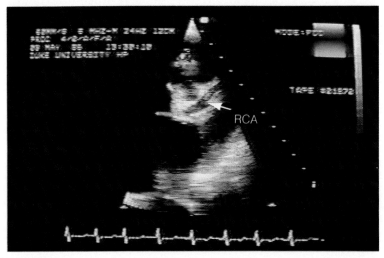

Fig. 12–6. Short-axis view of the aortic root showing flow in a portion of the right coronary artery. An enhanced map was used; spatial filters are on. This image was obtained from videotape and therefore is somewhat different in quality from images in other chapters.

permost on the image, with the cardiac apex furthest away. The left ventricle may appear somewhat foreshortened, as the ultrasound beam cannot always be directed precisely through the apex.

When the imaging plane is directed more anteriorly from the same position behind the left atrium, the great vessels and the atria will appear. The interatrial septum, lying at right angles to the ultrasound beam, can also be very well defined. Likewise, the aortic valve is imaged in cross section and the aortic root can be examined. Interestingly, coronary arteries and coronary artery flows are frequently seen using this transesophageal approach. Figure 12–5 demonstrates flow in the proximal portion of the left coronary artery. Figure 12–6 demonstrates some flow in the right coronary artery.

Development of Transesophageal Echo

Since early work done by Frazin in 1976 with an M-mode transducer[1] and by Matsumoto who used a mechanically rotated scanner,[2,3] there are now available phased array transducers for two-dimensional imaging and color flow mapping incorporated in a flexible gastroscope. In 1982, Schluter[4] and coworkers first reported the use of two-dimensional imaging with a phased array transducer in 26 awake patients, leading several other investigators to explore the clinical value of transesophageal imaging.

At first presentation of this approach, most readers are likely to imagine the procedure rather traumatic for the patient. Remember that the techniques of insertion and manipulation of the probe are very similar to those of standard endoscopy employed by gastroenterologists many times each day in ambulatory patients.

The tip of the gastroscope can be flexed and angled by use of the two external controls, which allows the operator to obtain different imaging planes from the esophagus. Diagnostic transesophageal imaging in the awake patient requires topical anesthesia for the pharynx; patients are held fasting for 8 hours prior to the procedure but do not necessarily require any premedication. For example, 50 to 100 mg of 10 percent lidocaine spray has been found very satisfactory. Extensive experience in both awake and anesthetized patients has confirmed the safety of this technique. There have been no reports of esophageal trauma, and with appropriate local anesthesia, patients have tolerated the procedure very well.

Transesophageal Doppler

Using conventional pulsed Doppler echocardiography, Schluter has already demonstrated that the sensitivity and specificity of transesophageal imaging for the detection of mitral regurgitation is far superior to that of transthoracic imaging.[5] Similarly, it has been proven very useful for the detection of shunts through atrial septal defects, and there are a few reports of aortic aneurysms transesophageal, but not transthoracic, imaging.[6] Since Doppler color flow mapping has become available with the transesophageal transducer, these earlier promising clinical applications have continued to grow.

In anesthetized patients undergoing cardiac surgery, Doppler color flow mapping allows evaluation of intracardiac blood flow immediately before and after surgical repairs. In our own experience, this has resulted in the correction of preoperative diagnoses and in the identification of regurgitation persisting after valvular replacement. Our experience with intraoperative color flow imaging has been limited to date. Following, however, is a discussion that exemplifies the utility of this approach during surgical intervention.

Mitral Regurgitation

Many patients with coronary artery disease have mitral regurgitation at angiography. Often this is felt to be catheter-induced and not clinically significant. We have found, in five of seven patients having coronary artery bypass grafting, at least some evidence of mitral regur-

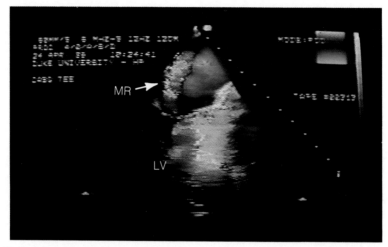

Fig. 12–7. Mitral regurgitation, previously undiagnosed, in a patient undergoing coronary artery bypass grafting. Note that the regurgitant jet is in hues of red, in contrast to transthoracic color flow mapping, because the transducer is located behind the heart. An enhanced map was used; spatial filters are on. This image was obtained from videotape and therefore is somewhat different in quality from images in other chapters.

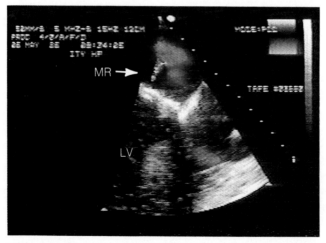

Fig. 12–8. Minor amount of perivalvular mitral regurgitation between two sutures of a freshly implanted valve bioprosthesis. An enhanced map was used; spatial filters are on. This image was obtained from videotape and therefore is somewhat different in quality from images in other chapters.

gitation visible by Doppler color flow mapping. One such example of mitral insufficiency is demonstrated in Figure 12–7. In all cases, mitral regurgitation was not clinically suspected and had not been observed at angiography. No patient had a v-wave on the pulmonary artery wedge pressure tracing at the time of intraoperative imaging. It appears, therefore, that Doppler color flow mapping is extremely sensitive and may detect mitral regurgitation in many patients in whom it is clinically insignificant. Indeed it has been reported that regurgitation through a 1-mm orifice can be detected by Doppler color flow mapping.[7]

Clinically significant mitral regurgitation appears as a narrow, mosaic colored jet of blood flow extending far back into the left atrium, sometimes into the pulmonary veins. This is in sharp contrast to the paravalvular leaks which we have seen immediately following mitral valve replacement, where a small jet of flow may appear intermittently from the mitral valve annulus, adjacent to the prosthetic valve (Fig. 12–8). Omoto has found that such leaks, apparent immediately after surgery, have disappeared by 2 weeks postoperatively, suggesting that small suture line leaks are obliterated during the healing process, and do not constitute grounds for revision of the annular attachment of the valve.

Intracardiac Masses

The history, transthoracic color flow images, and operative findings on a woman with left atrial myxoma were presented in Chapter 11. At the time of surgery, intraoperative transesophageal imaging revealed some mitral regurgitation occurring around the myxoma, which abutted against the anterior mitral valve leaflet (Fig. 12–9). It was also densely adherent to the interatrial septum, which required extensive resection, removal, and replacement with a pericardial patch graft.

Following removal from cardiopulmonary bypass, significant mitral regurgitation persisted (Fig. 12–10). A decision for further surgical repair of the mitral valve was rejected on the assumption that the mitral regurgitation would decrease over time.

There was also evidence of a small jet of blood flow crossing the interatrial septum from right to left near the roof of the coronary sinus. Figure 12–11 demonstrates a glimpse of this tiny shunt. The remainder of the suture line of the pericardial patch graft appeared intact and was without apparent leak. Such small suture line leaks may occur much more often than has been recognized previously. The patient successfully recovered from the surgical procedure and was noted to have trivial mitral regurgitation 6 days postoperatively.

Transesophageal approaches frequently reveal findings impossible to obtain from the chest wall, particularly when transthoracic image quality is impaired by lung disease, advanced patient age, or any other reason. Figure 12–12 reveals the right atrial mass lesion that was quite difficult to image from the chest wall in the second intraoperative case described in detail in Chapter 11. Note that the mass lesion is readily identified.

Aortic Aneurysm with Dissection

Dissecting aortic aneurysm is frequently quite difficult to image from the chest wall. Figure 12–13 illustrates the transesophageal color flow image of the short axis of the aortic root from a patient with a Type I ascending aortic aneurysm dissection in which the ascending aorta can be seen to be massively dilated. Image quality from the chest wall was exceedingly poor in this patient, and only a dilated aorta could be confirmed. An intimal flap was clearly seen by transesophageal echocardiography, separating the true lumen from the false lumen, and a defect in the intimal flap suggested a possible point of communication between the two. Color imaging confirmed flow of blood across the intimal tear identified by conventional two-dimensional imaging. A mosaic resulting from marked aliasing is seen in the true lumen. Marked aortic insufficiency was also seen ex-

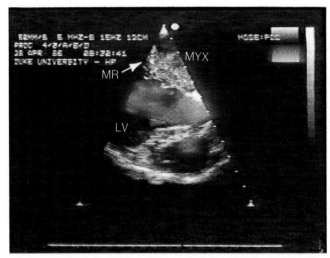

Fig. 12–9. Mitral regurgitation around a left atrial myxoma. The myxoma measured 8 cm in diameter and protruded into the right atrium through the foramen ovale. The clinical history and other echo findings on this patient were described in Chapter 11. An enhanced map was used; spatial filters are on. This image was obtained from videotape and therefore is somewhat different in quality from images in other chapters.

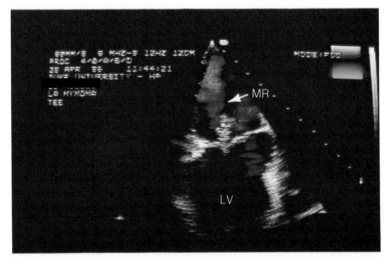

Fig. 12–10. Persistent mitral regurgitation immediately following the removal of the left atrial myxoma shown in Figure 12–9. This disappeared by 6 days postsurgery. An enhanced map was used; spatial filters are on. This image was obtained from videotape and therefore is somewhat different in quality from images in other chapters.

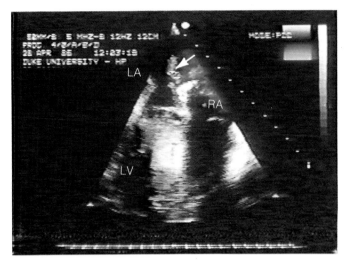

Fig. 12–11. Small right-to-left shunt (arrow) at one of the edges of the pericardial patch in the patient with left atrial myxoma deemed to be clinically insignificant. An enhanced map was used; spatial filters are on. This image was obtained from videotape and therefore is somewhat different in quality from images in other chapters.

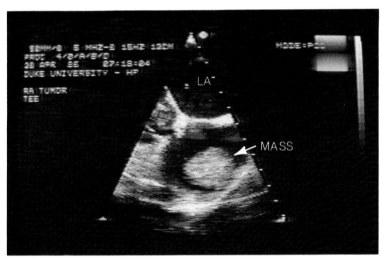

Fig. 12–12. Transesophageal color flow study readily showing a right atrial mass (arrow). This mass was not well seen from the transthoracic approach. Note how well the interatrial septum is seen stretching from left to right across the scan plane. An enhanced map was used; spatial filters are on. This image was obtained from videotape and therefore is somewhat different in quality from images in other chapters.

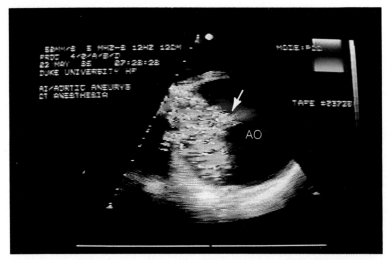

Fig. 12–13. Transesophageal color flow echocardiogram of a grossly dilated aortic root in a patient with a Type I aortic aneurysm. Flow is seen to move through an intimal tear into the false lumen (arrow). An enhanced map was used; spatial filters are on. This image was obtained from videotape and therefore is somewhat different in quality from images in other chapters.

tending toward the apex of the left ventricle.

General experience with transesophageal color flow imaging is currently limited to only a few institutions. Early indications are, however, that image quality is quite good and that it is possible to obtain information in most cases when the results of transthoracic studies are indeterminate. Moreover, its use during surgical interventions provide a means to acquire new knowledge about the approach to surgical repair and assessing the adequacy of surgical interventions.

References

1. Frazin L, Talano JV, Stephanides L, Loeb HS, Kopel L, Gunnar RM: Esophageal echocardiography. Circulation 54:102–108, 1976
2. Matsumota M, Hanrath P, Kremen P, Tamo C, Langenstein BA, Schluter M, Weiter R, Bleifeld W: Evaluation of left ventricular performance during supine exercise by transesophageal M-mode echocardiography in normal subjects. Br Heart J 48:61–66, 1982
3. Matsumoto M, Oka Y, Strom J, Frishman W, Kadish A, Becker RM, Frater RWM, Soneblic EH: Application of transesophageal echocardiography to continuous intraoperative monitoring of left ventricular performance. Am J Cardiol 46:95–105, 1980
4. Schluter M, Langenstein BA, Polster J, Kremer P, Souquet J, Engel S, Hanrath P: Transesophageal cross-sectional echocardiography with a phased array transducer system: technique and initial clinical results. Br Heart J 48:67–72, 1982
5. Schluter M, Langenstein BA, Hanrath P, Kremer P, Bleifeld W: Assessment of transesophageal pulsed Doppler echocardiography in the detection of mitral regurgitation. Circulation 66:784–789, 1982
6. Borner N, Erbet R, Braun B, Henkel B, Meyer J, Rumpelt J: Diagnosis of aortic dissection by transesophageal echocardiography. Am J Cardiol 54:1157–1158, 1984
7. Switzer DF, Nanda NC: Doppler color flow mapping. Ultrasound in Med and Biol 11:403–416, 1985

Appendix:
List of Abbreviations

AO = aortic root
AI = aortic insufficiency
AS = aortic stenosis
ASD = atrial septal defect
AV = aortic valve
BS = Bjork-Shiley prosthesis
CE = Carpentier-Edwards prosthesis
CS = coronary sinus
LA = left atrium
LPA = left pulmonary artery
LV = left ventricle
IVC = inferior vena cava
MPA = main pulmonary artery
MR = mitral regurgitation
MS = mitral stenosis
MV = mitral valve
MVR = mitral valve replacement
PA = pulmonary artery
PI = pulmonic insufficiency
PS = pulmonic stenosis
PV = pulmonary vein
RA = right atrium
RPA = right pulmonary artery
RV = right ventricle
RVOT = right ventricular outflow tract
SE = Starr-Edwards prosthesis
SVC = superior vena cava
TR = tricuspid regurgitation
TS = tricuspid stenosis
TV = tricuspid valve
TVR = tricuspid valve replacement
VSD = ventricular septal defect

Index

Page numbers followed by *f* indicate figures; those followed by *t* indicate tables.